FINDING YOUR

AFTER 50

Copyright - 2008

This book is dedicated to
my amazing daughters,
Molly and Libby.

CONTENTS

Acknowledgments ix
Introduction 1

PART ONE

LaterDating™: "A terrible thing happened again last night... nothing." Phyllis Diller

One	Find Yourself Alone? There is Hope.	5
Two	Our Lives Alone: Fulfilling or Empty?	11
Three	Your Dating Strategies Need to Change	15
Four	Writing a Book About Us LaterDaters™ Becomes Necessary	19

PART TWO

Two hundred LaterDaters™ speak up: "I have such poor vision I could date anybody." Gary Shandling

Five	Are You Having Fun Yet?	27
Six	What Qualities are You Seeking?	41
Seven	What are the Most Effective Methods for Meeting People to Date?	57
Eight	What Kind of Relationships are LaterDaters™ Seeking?	73

PART THREE

LaterDating™ Tips: "A man can sleep around, no questions asked, but if a woman makes nineteen or twenty mistakes, she's a tramp." Joan Rivers

Nine	Would You Date You?	89
Ten	Flirting	97
Eleven	Dating Dilemmas I Have Encountered and You May Too	103
Twelve	Why and How to Say "Good-Bye"	115
Thirteen	Better Living Through Chemistry	123
Fourteen	STDs, Yes, This Means You	131

PART FOUR

Your LaterDating™ Plan: "Even if you're on the right track, you'll get run over if you just sit there." Will Rogers

Fifteen	Your Dating Plan	135
Appendix	Expanded Information on Tables 7.2 and 7.3	141
Bibliography		143
About The Author		147

ACKNOWLEDGMENTS

It takes a lot of people to write a book. Putting words in a row is difficult, but it would have been impossible without the encouragement and advice from many people.

The memories of my wonderful marriage to Scott encouraged me to help other LaterDaters™ find happiness.

Paul Santo deserves a brilliant idea award for suggesting that I collect information from many other people who, like myself, were over fifty and attempting to date.

My daughters, Molly and Libby, kept telling me not to quit despite re-write after re-write. Molly's knowledge of surveys and statistics help make this book unique. Libby's addition of the word LaterDater™ to my book just might define us to the world.

A special thanks to all of the 235 people who took time to anonymously complete the survey and share their dating stories for use in the book. Those of you who have been asking about its progress can finally see your input in print.

More thanks go to my friends. They patiently listened to my endless, and probably boring, talk about how the book was coming along.

My sweetie, Jim, not only gave great editorial advice, but used that encouraging phrase—a good read.

My heartfelt thanks also go to my editors and publishers at Expert Publishing, Harry and Sharron Stockhausen. The intricacies of publishing and those apostrophes, dashes, and such would have been the death of me without their help.

INTRODUCTION

Romance offers people the closeness they desire. This desire doesn't disappear after the age of fifty. Remember your last loving relationship: kind words, a back rub, a leisurely walk, sharing the cooking, an unexpected gift? If we are over fifty and want a loving relationship in our lives, we have joined millions of others who could be termed LaterDaters™.

LaterDater™ (la–ter–da–ter) n. pl. s., A single person who dates later in life, i.e., after the age of fifty. Forty million people in the United States are potential members of this new demographic group.

If you are over fifty and thinking about joining the dating world, you may be experiencing the same feelings of insecurity you felt in high school. It seems many LaterDaters™ would prefer to avoid the social unease of dating altogether, but it is the necessary ritual before the dance of romance can begin. The power of positive thinking is not enough to make LaterDating™ enjoyable. You need to know where to find someone acceptable to date. Do you know how to flirt? You need to know what qualities people are looking for in a potential romantic interest. Are you a good date? You need to know what kind of relationship you are attempting to achieve by dating. How do you say good-bye to someone who doesn't share your relationship goals?

The information collected in this book comes from hundreds of single people over the age of fifty and will help you write your own plan for dating success. The statistics and the stories in this book will give you a clear picture of what you need to do to re-enter the dating world with confidence.

Chapter fifteen, at the end of this book, is your own dating plan. The first four chapters will get you ready to write that personal plan. These chapters explain that you, like the other forty million single people over the age of fifty, may need to adjust your rusty dating skills. The next four chapters give you the information taken from hundreds of surveys. This input should enable you to stop floundering around on the Internet and get a real dating life. Chapters nine and ten will help you turn the first date into a second and third date. Chapters eleven and twelve may save you from relationships that are more trouble than they are worth. Chapters thirteen and fourteen deal frankly with sexual intimacy as we age.

What's the worst that can happen? This book will empower you to design your own dating strategies. Stop listening to your insecurities and start planning for success. We LaterDaters™ are easy to find. There are forty million single people over the age of fifty in the United States and most of us want to have a date next Saturday night–how about you?

PART ONE

LaterDating™

"A terrible thing happened again last night... nothing."
Phyllis Diller

CHAPTER ONE

♥

Find Yourself Alone? There is Hope.

My Story

"Dial 9-1-1" was all he said to me. What was wrong with him? We'd been watching TV only ten minutes before. My husband, Scott, was only fifty-four, not old, not overweight, not a sick guy. His humor could capture a room and had entertained our family and me for fourteen years. We were building a cabin together so our future grandchildren would want to visit us when we retire. Together we imagined a wonderful life with an ever-expanding extended family.

At least six firemen tromped up the stairway. I took them to Scott who was sitting on the tile floor in the bathroom. They had all their fire gear on, but they didn't seem in a hurry. I was told to leave, but my heart was there with them. I knew that he was in big trouble. My daughter Libby was holding me as I leaned against the dining room wainscoting. She kept telling me not to worry, that Scott would be okay. When I asked one of the firemen what was wrong with my husband, he matter-of-factly replied, "Cardiac arrest." Five minutes later, I asked how he was doing. I was told, "Worse." To me a cardiac arrest becoming worse only meant one thing—Scott was dying.

The ambulance medics finally got there and went through their routine gestures. My daughter Molly drove me to the hospital. I tried to follow the medics into the hospital emergency room, but was told I had to wait in a special waiting room. This room soon filled up with the five adult children that made up our blended family, Aunt Nan, and Scott's first wife. We were hopeful and hugged each other, but were so quiet we could hear ourselves breathing. I was mute, numb from the shock, and leaning against the wall to support myself. Somehow, I already knew that Scott was dead.

When the emergency room staff entered our room to officially announce what I already knew, my only response was, "He's going to miss all the fun." Our marriage had been a wonderful chaos—five kids in college, big house, small dog, white cat, and gray rabbit pile of fun. We both enjoyed the constant activity. He had left all this behind, all our wonderful family and all our future plans. He had also left me.

In the other room, Scott waited. We were allowed to see him and say our good-byes. I stroked his hair and told him, "Don't worry. I will take care of you." Did I really think we would continue to take care of each other? Our life together was behind us now.

I'm not the only person who has lost a spouse through death or divorce, but at the time, when we go through the experience, we feel like we're the only ones. None of us can imagine that anyone else has felt such a deep sense of loss. The pain is an angry pain. When I saw very elderly people on the sidewalk or in a store, I would ask why not them, why aren't they dead—instead of my fifty-four-years-young husband? Seeing happy couples only made my feeling of abandonment more intense.

We all respond to the loss of a sweetheart differently. I needed to be the first person to speak at Scott's funeral. So many people loved this man. He was able to make anyone feel happy. The funeral home was packed beyond its capacity. People stood in the aisles. My wonderful women friends served a buffet for hundreds of people that filed through our home. We drank Scotch and attempted to comfort one another.

I couldn't eat or sleep. I finally got the right type of sleeping pills, but not until I had lost twenty pounds. My children said I looked like a stick with a head on top. I sold the beautiful house I'd lived in for thirty years because I couldn't imagine being there without Scott walking through the door and delivering his 1950s TV line, "Honey, I'm home." My normally positive attitude disappeared. Friends and relatives came around for a while, but grief doesn't make for good dinner conversation. Life was a lonely place, made lonelier by my new status as a single person.

The Bigger Story

Although some people become widows or widowers, the much more common reason for being single after fifty is divorce. Deirdre Bair in *Calling It Quits: Late-Life Divorce And Starting Over*, studies the surprising increase in late-life divorces around the world. She interviewed hundreds of people who have decided to divorce after thirty, forty, fifty, or even more years of marriage. Couples don't always grow closer as they age because people change and children leave. Sometimes we become intolerant of our spouses' faults and decide to make a new life for ourselves. This split may be easier on the dumper than on the dumpee, but no matter how the divorce story begins, at the end, there are two more single people over the age of fifty.

All of us who are single know that we are the odd chairs at the table. Many of us have spent our adult life in a world of couples. The world likes even numbers. Single men are usually more welcome into the couples' world than single women. The coupled women who make the dinner plans are more likely to invite a recently divorced or widowed gentleman over the age of fifty as a nice care-taking gesture. They want to make sure the single guy has a good meal. On the other hand, single women over the age of fifty do their own cooking at home, alone. Maybe these coupled women perceive single women as possible threats to their own cozy couple state. Men who are newly single after the age of fifty usually don't get enough support from their guy buddies—either married or single. There seems to be macho behavior patterns between men that exclude care-taking one another. My male friends tell me that they don't go to movies or out to dinner with their buddies because they think they'll be perceived as gay. We hear men using phrases like "Good shot," "Great job," and "You getting any?" How often do they say, "I'm so sorry to hear about your divorce. I imagine you're feeling pain. If you need someone to talk to, please call"?

Both older single men and women usually attempt to continue a healthy social life by finding other single individuals who share common interests with them. We all know that *Home Alone* was a cute movie, but most people don't choose it as a lifestyle.

Here we are as single people, alone and hurting, and we want the comfort that is offered by both our individual and couple friends. Those of us who had great marriages or long-term relationships are often anxious to find a new source of friendship or intimacy. Even those of us who had to bear the pain of a nasty divorce usually hope to find the right one the next time. We may be fifty, or sixty, or seventy, but one thing is sure—we are not dead. Most of us want to spend the remaining years of our life in a loving relationship. We are looking for a new beginning.

It soon becomes clear that finding a new, loving relationship is nearly impossible without participating in the adult dating world. Just the word "dating" frightens many adults. Some would compare it to having an IED duct taped to their chest. It is my hope that this book will guide you from fear to fun in your perceptions about dating.

This dating world is very different from the one we encountered twenty, thirty, or forty years ago. Whether your goal is simple companionship or marriage, surviving the current dating world and finding the right person are challenging. This book was written to offer support in this process by providing you with advice from people in similar situations, people over fifty and dating. This book is also designed to engage you in charting your own plan, with easy-to-follow steps, and advice for successfully navigating the adult dating world.

If you are a single man or woman over fifty who is seeking a relationship, you are not alone. You're one of about forty million people in the United States that is qualified to join the LaterDater's™ group. I've been in this group for some time now. During these years I've dated a lot, laughed a lot, cried a lot, and learned a great deal. I have also heard the comment, "You should really write a book," from my family, married friends, and other single people. My single friends kept asking where to meet single people over fifty, while my married friends and my family have enjoyed my dating stories over the years. Maybe they thought a book project would help slow down my fast-paced dating life. I, too, needed a helpful book about how to be successful at dating, but I was too busy dating to write one.

You, dear reader, and I are experiencing something that has never before happened in the history of mankind—senior dating. I've decided to call us the LaterDaters™ because most of us don't like the word senior unless it saves us money at the movies or golf course. During our lifetimes we have experienced the dating world, and now we're ready to try it again. We're older and wiser now, but we may need some help in returning to this new dating world after the age of fifty.

According to the U.S. Census Bureau, in 2005, there were 13 1/2 million single men over the age of forty-five in this country (U.S. Census Bureau, 2005, Table 55). Single women over the age of forty-five outnumber men by a long shot—at twenty-four million. The Census Bureau doesn't publish the numbers for single people over the age of fifty, but you get the idea. When these numbers are added together, there are more than 37 1/2 million of us. We are either divorced, widowed, separated, or never married. Like me, many have fallen into more than one of these categories over our lifetimes. Some of us LaterDaters™ have lived through the pain of multiple divorces, or the death of more than one spouse.

Our LaterDater™ group is part of a larger and growing crowd—The Baby Boomers, who are hitting their sixties. The younger end of that demographic is approaching fifty. It is estimated that one quarter of the U.S. population is surging toward their sixties. Those of us born between 1946 and 1964 are considered the Boomers, and there are seventy-seven million of us. Many of this seventy-seven million will, hopefully, remain happily married forever, but the divorce rate and death statistics predict that many of us—at some point—will experience being single. Some of us want to remain single, but most of us want a new love in our life.

The millions of single people over the age of fifty can't be ignored. Many of us would like to date someone or even get married again. If you are one of these people, you've probably experienced more than a little frustration and disappointment in your search for companionship. Some of you may have given up on attempting to date because you don't know where to start, or you tried it and found the process can be painful.

Dating, at any age, is a relatively recent activity. Arranged marriages are still the norm in many places around the world. Until the last one hundred years, family agreements and practical pairings were the most common way to meet a mate in the United States—and that was for young folks. When the agriculture economy dominated our country, barn dances were popular meeting places for young people. My parents met at a barn dance and they went on to marry and have a family. I'm sure they never imagined that their youngest daughter would be in the dating world at the age of sixty-one. The relative lack of mobility, rural isolation, a divorce rate that was much lower than today's 50 percent, and a shorter life span made dating over the age of fifty a rarity.

And LaterDating™ is even a newer chapter in dating history. In 1950, only 10 percent of people over fifty lived in single-person households, but by 2003, 26 percent of us were living alone (Frances 2003). If we look back fifty years, we may remember a few divorced people and a few widows or widowers. Some of these rare few may have met another single adult at church and started a dating relationship. Maybe you remember some, but I don't remember a single one. The high divorce rate, the huge number of Baby Boomers, better health care, and the new drugs that enhance sexual appetite in women and sexual performance in men have changed the adult dating landscape from a small field to a panoramic vista. I'm not overstating the current LaterDating™ world by using the words new social phenomenon.

Let's face it, if you're over fifty and attempting to date, you're a twenty-first century pioneer. This significant historical movement is overlooked because we're right in the middle of it. In the 1996 book, *The Graying of America: an Encyclopedia of Aging, Health, Mind, and Behavior,* by Donald H. Kaiser and Barry C. Kausler, the authors totally ignored the dating behavior of older Americans. The word arousal is used to explain how quickly we become angry. The states of divorce and widowhood are mentioned without any reference to resumption of dating and seeking a new mate. The only hint that there might be some coupling in later life is a statement that says elderly men are more likely to remarry than elderly women. It's hard to believe, even insulting, that we had an entire encyclopedia written about us and it has ignored the forty million of us who are single and the fact that many of us are looking for a sweetheart. You can almost hear the Boomers adding their huge numbers to this parade every day.

If you are alone and want this state to change, there's hope—lots of hope.

CHAPTER TWO

Our Lives Alone: Fulfilling or Empty?

A little introspection never hurt anyone. Try and answer the question that begins chapter two: Is your life alone fulfilling or empty? Are you enjoying single life? Does there seem to be some space left over in your day? Careers, friends, children, hobbies, pets, and travels can fill up your life. My friends tell me that having grandchildren is the equivalent to winning the lottery of a lifetime. In chapter eight of this book you will see that 26 percent of the women and 14 percent of the men who took my survey declared that they were "single and loving it." That leaves the rest of us. We're the ones who have an empty place in our lives that we would like to fill with someone we could call our Valentine.

Let's imagine that it's the end of January and the day dedicated to the heart, Valentine's Day, is coming. No matter what your age, it's not a good time to be single. You may be thinking—even obsessing—about your dating life. Hopefully, you have fond memories of mushy Valentine cards, chocolates, and flowers. I have a wonderful memory from my marriage of a certain Valentine's Day when the Christmas tree was still up in our living room. I took off the decorations and covered the tree with red paper hearts with those candy heart words, "Be mine," "I love you," "You're cute." After placing our dinner table next to that very dry tree, I served my dear husband a candlelight dinner. We kidded about why neither of us had taken the tree out of our house. We imagined using it as an Easter tree, a Memorial Day tree, and a birthday tree. He gave me a book of love stories inscribed with the words, "Someday they will write about our love story." Stories like this one are the stuff our fondest memories are made of. Being with someone you love on Valentine's Day is what most of us want.

Like you, I now live alone. I live in a condo and don't bother with a tree. I was invited to a Women's Valentine's Day Party, but I had to decline. I'm spending Valentine's Day with a wonderful man at a romantic club. He's not the same man with whom I spent last Valentine's Day. I'm sharing this information with you because you need to know it's possible to have many romantic days in your future. Your age is not a barrier to romance. The reason for this happy fact is that there are millions of other single people close to your age who are also looking for romance.

Remember, there are about forty million of us in the United States who are over fifty and single. As our kids would say, "You are s-o-o not alone." We can't be ignored because we're everywhere. And we're healthier and wealthier than the generations that came before us. We've suffered loss through death or divorce, but we are able to find love again because there are literally millions of us, and we can drive, fly, and email around and across the entire country to find it. In the past, a single person over fifty would have been lucky to marry the farmer, or the farmer's widow on the neighboring farm. But, here's the good news—we now have the ability to meet and go out with at least a few hundred of those forty million people.

Today, as single people, we don't have to be lonely because we cannot only fill time with our work, causes, hobbies, friends, and relatives, but with our dates. I realized long ago that I love to be with other people. Alone, I grieve too much and bore myself. I need feedback, even if that feedback is a "ha ha" at one of my dumb jokes. My female friends are great fun, my adult daughters are delightful, but I also want to date because dating is fun and an essential ritual that can lead me to that special person. Sharing your life with the right person is a sure cure for loneliness, and it's also a great recipe for many future happy Valentine's Days.

CHAPTER TWO 13

Living in a coupled relationship gives us even more than love and company. Recent medical findings have concluded that loneliness is bad for your health. James J. Lynch, Ph.D., in his book, *A Cry Unheard: New Insights into the Medical Consequences of Loneliness*, has uncovered a startling connection between the loss of social support in adulthood and damage to cardiovascular health. We could conclude from Dr. Lynch's book that happy Valentine's Days are heart-healthy events.

At this time in your life, you may be settled into living alone. Your routine is just the way you like it, and the bathroom cabinets and the closet finally seem to be big enough. Cooking has become optional and can mean just about any method or menu. My daughters have teased me about making a dinner out of chocolate covered coffee beans. It works for me. I sometimes cook a large quantity of something to freeze in individual servings. These servings always end up freezer burned. Even though we singles can still rattle those pots and pans, all the single people I know say, "It isn't any fun to cook for just one." They agree that food is so much more enjoyable when shared with family, friends, or a sweetheart.

I have trouble believing singles when they say they don't want a sweetheart in their lives. Why don't we just admit that we're herd animals? We don't like going to movies or restaurants alone. We'll go to coffee shops alone, but only if we can look busy on our computers. Fifty-one percent of women in the United States live alone. I'm not too proud to admit that I'm one of them, and that I hate living alone.

I love sharing my pot of coffee and newspaper outrage with someone who'll put his finger on the spot he's reading and listen to my babble before returning to where he left off. I enjoy planning meals and social events that I think my partner will enjoy. While I'm standing in the kitchen, those kisses on the back of my neck are glorious. Watching a movie with someone I love is much more fun because I can share the humor of the comedies and the fright of the horror flicks.

For anyone who's been hurt by bad relationships, I hope you'll find that special person who can make you laugh again. Maybe you'll even want to cook, dance, and risk loving someone again. Friday and Saturday night with the remote control is safe—but sad and lonely for the majority of us. Do you want to change your single status into a coupled relationship? Keep reading, because the rest of the book is devoted to helping each and everyone of you find your sweetie.

CHAPTER THREE

♥

Your Dating Strategies Need to Change

Shopping for a Sweetheart

Take a moment and imagine dating as a form of comparison shopping. Some people only have enough energy to go to two different stores; others realize that choosing a mate is one of the most important decisions they make in a lifetime. Haven't we all noticed the differences between women shoppers and men shoppers? I see women going to many stores and looking at many different pairs of shoes, styles of chairs, or types of cell phones before they make a decision. On the other hand, men usually go to their favorite store, buy their usual brand, and go home. I've read that when people marry for the first time, they typically choose the person from their third serious relationship. Dear reader, this is not a sufficient market survey.

We LaterDaters™, in this new world of easy transportation and communication, can, at the least, be more thorough in our dating adventures. I understand that some don't want to spend time and energy on finding the right person. So you take one of two dead ends. You quickly choose the wrong person, or choose to remain single. Even if you avoid these two options, other troublesome behavior patterns can emerge. Men, playing the role of caveman hunters, can move too quickly, see their prey, and go after it—no matter if it's the same golf shirt in five different colors or someone to date. Women, playing the role of cave woman gatherers, tend to shop at a variety of stores overanalyzing and comparing many suitable partners.

Both men and women can also fall prey to a problem similar to attributing qualities to a product because of its brand name. For example, a man can meet a beautiful woman and attribute other qualities to her just because he is attracted to her beauty. He may describe her as witty, hardworking, creative, and see numerous other wonderful qualities that she may not have. He is blindsided by her appearance. He will overlook the possible negatives in the lovely woman because lovely sells. Women are not immune to brand name shopping either. Women may overlook negative traits in a man if that man has money. It's easier to look for a sense of humor, kindness, and good health in a man who has already passed the financial stability hurdle. Both men and women can be too impressed by good looks and/or money in their dating lives. Chapter six will help us get our priorities straightened out on that.

Go Out with Many People—You're not in High School Anymore

Going out with many people can help us to avoid some of the pitfalls described above. When I first began dating, I took a lot of grief from my friends. After they asked me if I was dating anyone, they were stupefied when I named three or four people. I quickly explained that these were not intimate relationships. They still wanted to know how I met all these men, and how I kept them straight. So I told them—I kept a list by the phone. My philosophy was a bit unconventional to them, since they were people who had married their third serious sweetheart or they were lucky enough to have kept their spouse. My single lady friends were very curious about how I was doing all this dating. Most of them had given up on finding someone they even wanted to date. They went out with someone just one time, or even for a while, and then they were either dumped or they did the dumping.

The pattern was that they then sat home for six to twelve months until someone else appeared. (If someone else did appear.) These passive daters were repeating what they had done in high school and college. In those days of yore, everyone in school knew when and if you were going steady or were pinned. That meant you were not available for dating. This is how we ended up with very limited market surveys and that 50 percent divorce rate! This is precisely why I dated more than one gentleman at a time. Reader, if you get lucky and find the perfect match on your first adult dating experience, I'm envious of you. But you are in the minority. For the majority of us, going out with multiple people will help us to avoid the under and over analyzing pitfalls while we search for a good match.

Found that Special Person? Be Pro-active

When you are going out with lots of different people, the great date will finally happen. Think of it as a numbers game—maybe even gambling. You've played the game for a while and this time you were dealt a great hand in the form of a wonderful person. Be sure to play your cards correctly. Let that person know that you appreciate his or her good qualities. Yes, actually tell them what you find attractive about them—robust laugh, quick wit, sense of style. Be sure to exchange business cards. Don't have them? Get them. Call or email that wonderful person as soon as you can after that first meeting and suggest another date. Send flowers. I sent flowers to a man and he remembered it four years later. Everyone is flattered by being pursued in this way because we all have insecurities that desire compliments.

Dating and Sex are Two Different Activities

I can hear you saying "who is this crazy woman?" Dating many people at the same time and keeping a list of their names by the phone doesn't fit with most people's images of romance. You may be thinking that when you date someone, you will naturally be having sex with that person. I think you date for fun, and if and when a relationship develops into something that seems really good, you put away the list next to the phone and move that relationship to the next level. That's the level where you become intimate. A friend of mine told me she would never try dating using my system because she wanted to see someone across a crowded room and have sparks fly. This scenario is beautiful, but if it worked, there would be many more buildings on fire out there. Waiting for sparks is likely to be a long wait for the majority of us. What do we want to be doing in the meantime? How about dating for fun?

CHAPTER FOUR

Writing a Book About Us Later Daters™ Becomes Necessary

The Planets Align

While engaged in dating for fun, my dating adventures and misadventures began to pile up. Being someone who enjoys telling funny stories, I shared these adventures with my friends. Some of them bluntly told me I was going overboard, both on the dating and the stories about dating. Others said I should write a book. This seemed like a ridiculous idea because I wasn't famous. Katie Couric could write a book about dating, and someone would publish it in a snap. She could afford assistants, and her name on the cover would sell a book about dating, even if she had only dated five different men in her entire lifetime.

My decision to write a book about dating was made at my cabin in Wisconsin. I invited two couples for the weekend. Paul made his living as a writer, and I had a lot of respect for his talent. When I told him I didn't think anyone really cared about Linda Fraser's dating life, he suggested that I gather information from other single people's dating experiences. This seemed like a practical plan that would give me insight into the bigger picture of dating after the age of fifty. How to proceed with this gathering process was such a marvelous coincidence, that I felt this book *had* to be written.

The coincidence came in the form of my daughter, Dr. Molly Coyne, with her Ph.D. in Evaluation. When I told her about Paul's suggestion, she happened to be taking a course in survey design. She asked me what I wanted to learn in my survey and then proceeded to turn my rather vague ideas into a valid survey. Her survey would produce numbers that could be crunched (she said disaggregated) in her very fancy computer. It would also allow me to collect qualitative data, or stories and experiences, from other fifty-plus singles out there in the LaterDating™ world.

The Work Starts

Molly and I designed a survey to find out four things about singles over fifty:

1.) Are we enjoying dating?
2.) What qualities are we looking for in someone to date?
3.) What methods are working for us to meet dates?
4.) What kind of relationship are we hoping to achieve by dating?

I put the surveys in self-addressed stamped envelopes and hit the streets. I went to places where I knew there would be single people over fifty and told them what I was doing and how much I would appreciate their help. Yes, I even begged them to please fill out my survey and drop it into a mailbox. I handed out over 650 surveys to both men and women, and was surprised and delighted by the response I received. Over 235 people mailed their surveys back to me.

During the data-collection stage of writing this book, I needed to be assertive. I had to approach people I didn't know and talk them into spending their time on my project. They all wanted an explanation. Using smiles and a short explanation of my book idea, I was overwhelmed by the willingness of people to fill out a two-page survey, and even to write detailed stories about their dating experiences.

People Want Help

The question that kept me going to singles groups that meet in church basements, speed-dating events, singles dances, singles ski and tennis groups, and even to single strangers in bars to distribute surveys was this:

"What have you learned so far?"

This question was asked by nearly everyone. I didn't knock on doors and survey people who were united with their remote controls. The people who participated were curious single people over the age of fifty who were out there in the singles world. The people I surveyed were earnestly trying to meet other singles, and almost to a person, they asked that same question: "What have you learned so far?"

It began to sound like a cry for help. They were out there, trying to find a sweetie, but they wanted answers about how to find and attract the one special person that would make their lives more wonderful. I couldn't stop the process I had started and not share what they willingly shared with me. I owed them this book. They wanted to know "What have you learned so far?" and I'm going to tell them.

Who are These People?

You may be interested to know more about where I passed out my surveys and what demographic groups were included. I started in my own condo building of 107 units. Half of the residents are single people between fifty and ninety, well educated, and well off. The response from this group was very low. They feared I was invading their privacy because we all lived in the same place. I then went to a singles ski club and a singles tennis club and handed out my surveys to those who were over fifty. The members of these groups were up to sixty-five years old, physically active, with diverse educational backgrounds and incomes.

A speed-dating event for people over fifty allowed me to hand out forty more surveys to the participants who also covered the full spectrum of education and income.

I also surveyed a singles club for business and professional singles that had members who were over sixty-five and well to extremely well educated. Most of them were enjoying a financially comfortable retirement.

Singles dances were great places to get my surveys out and do some dancing too. These dances were attended by people with a wide range of education levels and incomes.

The largest singles group in my area that I surveyed meets in a church basement, but isn't affiliated with that church. This group has a low membership fee and provides low priced activities and events for singles between fifty and eighty. The variety of education and income demographics in this group is very wide, but many of them are on a more limited budget than the other groups I surveyed.

And, let's not forget those coffee shops and bars, where I handed out surveys to anyone over fifty and single who would take one.

The worst place I found to do survey work was on a date. These dates thought I'd gone out with them just to get more data. They felt like lab rats and they usually never asked me out again.

In summary, the majority of the singles I surveyed were:

1) Enjoying middle to high incomes in the Minneapolis—St. Paul metropolitan area.
2) Actively participating in a setting that could provide them with some dating possibilities.
3) Not given a survey to produce results that would prove one thing or another. I just wanted to find out and be able to share what's going on with singles over fifty.

Why this Book is the Way it is

The format I chose for this book is influenced by my work and educational background as a teacher with a Master's Degree in Curriculum Development. As you read this book, you will be asked to take the same survey that all of the people I surveyed took. You will be asked the same four questions:

1) How do you feel about dating?
2) What qualities do you want in the person you date?

3) What have you tried and what has actually worked for you to find people to date?
4) What type of relationship do you hope to achieve?

You will be given the tools to help you identify and achieve your personal relationship goal. You will be asked to draw some conclusions using your own responses and the information and stories in this book. Those conclusions will allow you to create your own personal plan for dating success.

When my surveys were collected and the data was crunched, it produced more data than I ever imagined. Statistics usually look like long lists of numbers. If you relate to numbers, you might appreciate that aspect of this book. However, many of us don't really want to know the difference between mean and median. I have tried to keep the math simple by using one hundred surveys from men and one hundred surveys from women, randomly selected from the 235 that were returned to me completed. I wanted to use percentages on the charts in this book that are easy to relate to actual people. Mark Twain said, "There are three types of lies—lies, damn lies, and statistics." With all due respect to Mr. Twain, the survey findings presented in this book are not manipulated in any way, but simply presented in summary tables to provide readers with useful information from fellow LaterDaters™.

In addition to the summary tables presenting responses to the four questions, this book includes the personal stories provided by the survey respondents. These stories both clarify and expand on the data in the tables, making it both more relevant and interesting. The surveys themselves included space for the LaterDaters™ to write about their experiences, and many of the people who took the survey were generous in sharing their stories of both outrageous and glorious dates. I am honored to be able to share these stories, and although the surveys were anonymous, I have eliminated or changed any identifying information. In addition to the rich data and stories, other research is noted where relevant. Some of my own stories and conclusions are also included.

PART TWO

TWO HUNDRED LATERDATERS™ SPEAK UP:

"I have such poor vision I can date anybody."
Gary Shandling

CHAPTER FIVE

Are You Having Fun Yet?

If you laughed at the title of this chapter, I'm guessing that dating is anything but fun for you. Dating should be an enjoyable social activity, but many of us think failure and rejection lurks behind every encounter. You may relate to the following letter.

Scared writes:

I haven't even attempted to find someone to date. I've been divorced for five years, and I'm fifty-seven years of age. My sons are now in college, and I think I might be ready for a relationship with someone who doesn't remind me of my ex. To be honest, I'm scared. My confidence was pretty much flushed down the drain in my divorce. Do I need to re-make myself, and how much will that cost? My job is fairly demanding, and I wonder if I have time to be in a relationship. In the worst case scenario, I see myself being sweet-talked by someone who has just declared bankruptcy, only to be dumped by the cad. So, all in all, I keep finding reasons not to get into a relationship, even though my life seems like it is missing something. What should I do?

Dear Scared:

This is my advice to you. Don't mortgage the farm for that cad. The good news is that chapter five will assure you that people your age who are dating are having fun doing it. You can get out there, have fun, and meet someone wonderful.
Happy dating, Linda

Dear reader, please take a minute and fill in the following check list to describe how you feel about dating. Of course, it is perfectly fine to have multiple feelings about dating, so go ahead and check away.

What words do you associate with dating? (check all that apply)

- ☐ Fun
- ☐ Intimidating
- ☐ Risky
- ☐ Time Consuming
- ☐ Expensive
- ☐ Disappointing

I asked two hundred survey respondents this same question. They were all single and over the age of fifty, and I learned a lot from their responses. Go ahead and answer this question yourself. Then read on and learn how others responded and what our responses might mean to our approaches to dating. Yes, use a pencil or pen because you will need to refer back to this section later. Don't skip this part. Which words would you associate most with dating?

If you had some trouble deciding which words to choose, you're not alone. Some of the people who responded to this survey question chose many words. If the word fun wasn't at least one of your choices, keep your spirits up; this book should be of help to you. Let's look at what might be behind each of these choices.

Fun

If you associated dating with fun, your definition of fun could mean anything from uproariously entertaining to just comfortable. Dating someone who has a similar sense of humor can lead to lots of shared laughter. Sharing a topic of interest might not lead to giggles, but it's certainly entertaining to talk with someone who is interested in some of the same things you are. Having fun on a date doesn't always mean witty repartee. Just feeling at ease with someone is often enough reason to be interested in a second or third date. If you did not select the word fun, using that very old rule of sociability—showing interest in a person's job, hobbies, children, and travels works on a date. Smiling at someone is usually mimicked back to you. We can all memorize a few jokes to share. Showing interest, smiling, and telling a few jokes can all lead to having fun on a date.

Intimidating

If you choose the word intimidating, you might be associating dating with rejection or other negative experiences of the past. When you check your self-esteem gauge, if the thought of even trying to date makes your mouth go dry, it's time to give yourself a pep talk. It may be helpful to keep in mind that there are no perfect people out there in the dating world. Why do you think you need to be a Hollywood star to deserve a date? Most of us are intimidated by someone who seems to be out of our league, i.e., smarter, richer, better looking, and more socially adept. Would your feelings of intimidation lessen if you attempted to date someone with a similar lifestyle as yours? If you're not sure what a similar lifestyle means, how about someone in your neighborhood or someone close to your own age? Finding people with whom we have things in common is bound to reduce feelings of intimidation.

Risky

The word risky could have many interpretations in the dating world. Some of you don't want to risk having your heart broken. Others don't want to risk intimacy because of sexually transmitted disease fears. If you have experienced physical or emotional abuse in a past relationship, you might see dating as a very real risk to your physical and mental health. As LaterDaters™, we are much better prepared for all the risks I've just mentioned. We're more logical than we were as emotionally-driven teenagers. Condoms are no longer kept behind the pharmacist's counter. Remember wondering who you could get to buy them for you? Surprise, you're legal now! Abuse is much less likely to be tolerated by an independent LaterDater™ than a young dependent person. The July/August 2005, *AARP: The Magazine* contained an article titled "Seeking Love." It contained the following statement: "According to the U.S. Census Bureau, being single later in life is becoming the norm. The one thing that our research continually shows is that the older a person gets, the more he/she becomes a practical dater, as opposed to being emotionally driven." We've all lived long and learned much. We can minimize the risk factors of dating.

Time Consuming

If you selected the phrase time consuming, it could mean that you have spent a lot of time looking for a potential date, or it could mean you've dated someone who wanted every minute of your life. Maybe you don't feel like you have time to get all gussied up to go out on the town on a regular basis. If your life is still full of children at home, a dog, a cat, and a sixty-hour workweek, it is understandable that you are short on time for dating. If any of these are the case, both on-line and off-line dating services may be just the help you need. They can be time-efficient and reduce time needed looking for someone to date. When you start going out with someone, it might be helpful to remember you aren't under any obligation to merge your life with that person's life simply because you are dating them. Starting a relationship with an explanation of your time constraints is not rude. It's honest.

Expensive

If you selected expensive, it could be that you are a woman who associated dating with the need for new clothing and trips to the beauty salon. Men selecting expensive may be thinking about $8.00 drinks and $75.00 tickets to see Jimmy Buffet. All these costs are in your control. Ladies are usually great comparison shoppers, and gentlemen can always suggest a walk/talk/picnic event instead of the big blowout dinner at a fancy restaurant. Not being wealthy is not a reason to avoid dating.

Disappointing

If you associated dating with the term disappointing, it may be your choice because you haven't had a date in the last year or more, or it could mean that the last forty-five people you went out with were all disappointing. Chapter ten on flirting should be of interest if you think you might be terminally dateless. Chapter twelve will help you if you are ignoring the red flags that should steer you clear of unsuitable dates.

What words do other LaterDaters™ associate with dating? Whatever your responses or your reasons, you need to know they are valid feelings. I have a good friend who is a great guy, single, and sixty-one years old. He describes dating as "feeling like a door-to-door salesman with yourself as the product." There aren't any right or wrong feelings when it comes to dating or salesmanship. Some of us will find dating fun; others of us will be intimidated. A few people will think it is risky, time consuming, and expensive. No matter what terms we associate with dating, all of us are likely to experience some disappointments along the way. For this reason, it might be helpful to keep in mind that we LaterDaters™ share these feelings. Table 5.1 shows how two hundred single men and women over the age of fifty responded to this same question.

What words do other LaterDaters™ use?

Table 5.1 on page 32 indicates that about half of the women and men who responded associated dating with the term fun. Fewer survey respondents associated dating with the terms intimidating, risky, time consuming, or expensive. Keep in mind that most of the respondents chose more than one term. Survey takers associated dating with a range of other terms or feelings. The numbers are low in the intimidation and risky columns, but in both cases, twice as many women chose this response as men. As far as dating time is concerned, 14 percent of men saw dating as time consuming, while 11 percent of women reported that feeling. No women reported dating as expensive, but only 8 percent of the men felt that way. The largest difference can be found in the word disappointing, because 27 percent of the women chose this word while only 14 percent of the men did.

It is important to note that the data does not necessarily represent the averages of the U.S. or any other population. The people who were surveyed were often found in places where they could probably meet someone to date, including singles dances, skiing clubs, etc. These men and women had not given up on the adult dating scene. They were, in

TABLE 5.1: TERMS ASSOCIATED WITH DATING BY GENDER

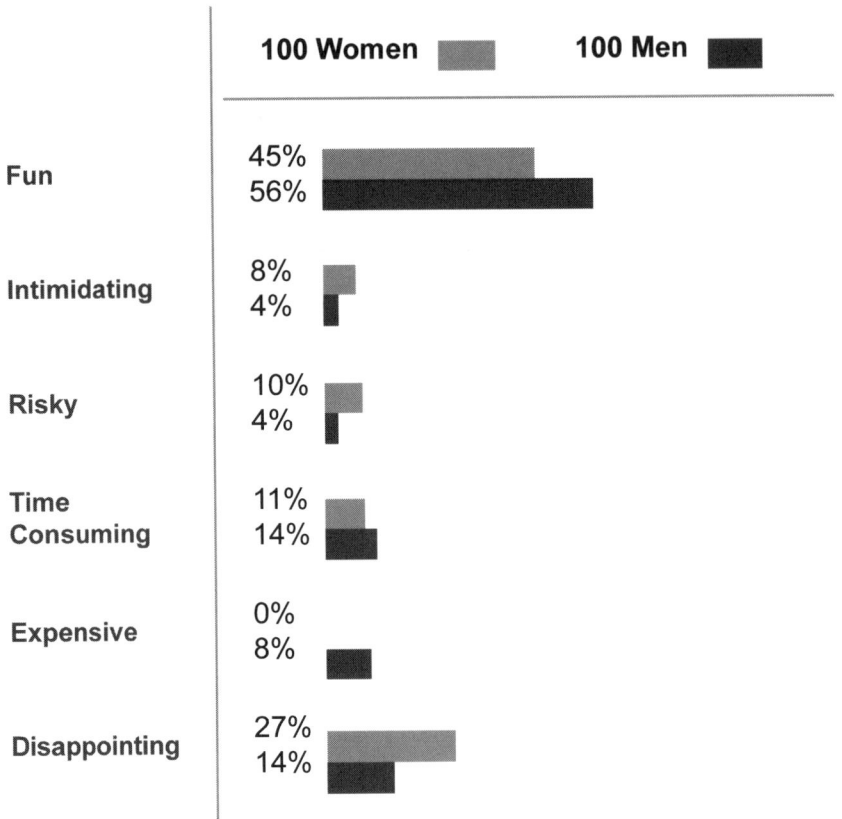

Note percentages do not total 100%, as some respondents selected more than one term.

places where they could meet future dates and their dating histories gave them plenty of opportunity to find dating fun, disappointing, expensive, etc. LaterDaters™ chose the word fun more frequently than any of the other choices. If you did not associate the word fun with dating, please keep reading.

Let's look at the survey again and examine how our age influences our enjoyment of dating. This will provide us with a more detailed understanding of just which surveyed people associated dating with fun. For example, was it mostly the youngest survey respondents who selected the term fun? You might be surprised to learn that it wasn't. In fact, it was the 71–75 age group that most often chose the word fun. See if other people in your age category associated dating with fun.

TABLE 5.2: PERCEPTIONS OF DATING BY AGE GROUPS

Ages ▶ Perceptions ▼	50-55 N=45	56-60 N=57	61-65 N=47	66-70 N=13	71-75 N=13	75+ N=8
Fun	44%	58%	66%	57%	**69%**	50%
Intimidating	11%	2%	2%	7%	15%	**25%**
Risky	7%	12%	0%	**13%**	8%	**13%**
Time Consuming	13%	12%	13%	**20%**	15%	13%
Expensive	4%	4%	2%	3%	8%	**25%**
Disappointing	33%	25%	21%	10%	8%	**36%**

N = number of respondents.
Some respondents chose more than one word.
Bold numbers show highest response rate.

Looking at the terms people associated with dating by age group produced some interesting results. It is important to note that the three oldest age groups are small. Fun was chosen by 69 percent of the thirteen people in the 71–75 age group. The fun choice had a close second in the 61–65 age group, with 66 percent of those forty-seven people choosing it. The youngest group (51–55) appears to be enjoying dating the least, with only 44 percent of you forty-five folks choosing Fun. Don't give up. Maybe you're just new at it. The fun of dating evidently increased with age. What a surprising gift.

No single age group seemed to be strongly negative about dating. The 61–65 age group didn't mention risky. The singles in the 66–70 age group had the highest reported percentage (20 percent) choosing the phrase time consuming. Twenty-five percent of the over 75 age group reported dating was expensive, but that was only two out of eight. It is interesting that the age groups most associating disappointment with dating were the youngest, and the oldest. Thirty-three percent of those in the 50–55 and 36 percent in the over 75 age group chose the term disappointing. Overall, finding dating fun does not seem to be a function of the age of the survey respondents. If you have been using age as a reason for dating disappointments, you might need to come up with a new reason. Apparently we can have fun dating at any age.

Find your age group and compare their answers to the answer you gave at the beginning of this chapter. Are other people in your age group feeling the same way you do about dating? If so, that's interesting. If not, it may give you a snapshot survey to assist you in hearing the feelings of other LaterDaters™.

Maybe you are like me and are thinking, "Hey, I have already been married twice. How many times have these survey respondents married? If they have been married multiple times, are they still finding dating fun? Let's take a look at the chart on the following page.

Chart 5.3 uses only the number of times survey respondents reported having been married to analyze their perceptions of dating. It indicates that slightly more than half of the 196 people who were never married or married one or two times associated dating with fun. In fact, the number of times respondents to my survey had been married did not seem to relate to how often they chose the word fun. The big surprise comes from the four people in our survey who had been married three times. All of them, 100 percent, thought dating was fun, and none of them associated dating with the term intimidating. Of course, it is important to note that only four of the survey takers reported having been married three times or more. Also, remember that some respondents chose more than one word to describe their dating perceptions, and that is why the math people are scratching their heads about the sum of the percentages in each row exceeding 100 percent.

Similar to the perceptions of the different age groups, the data show a nice consistent pattern in which number of times married does

TABLE 5.3: PERCEPTIONS OF DATING BY NUMBER OF TIMES MARRIED

Times Married ▶ Perceptions ▼	Married 0 times N=30	Married 1 time N=123	Married 2 times N=43	Married 3 times N=4
Fun	57%	55%	58%	**100%**
Intimidating	7%	7%	5%	0%
Risky	7%	8%	7%	25%
Time Consuming	17%	11%	21%	25%
Expensive	3%	2%	9%	25%
Disappointing	17%	4%	23%	25%

N = number of respondents.
Some respondents chose more than one word.
Bold numbers show highest response.

not seem to lead people to associate more or fewer negative terms with dating. "Fun" is still the winner. No matter whether a person has never been married or has been married more than once, half of us still associate the word fun with dating.

These data led me to think that most of us are willing to give new relationships a chance and that we can decide to not allow our past relationship disasters to spoil our views about starting new dating relationships. Approaching LaterDating™ with an open mind and letting go of past disappointments and negative stereotypes about members of the opposite sex will help all of us.

In addition to the questions asked, my survey invited Later Daters™ to share a personal dating story. I asked the survey respondents to write down their own thoughts, including outrageous, disastrous, wonderful, humorous, or romantic dating stories. My thanks to all of the generous people who were willing to share their dating adventures. Below are some of the wonderful statements and stories I recieved related to perceptions of dating.

Your Stories

Fun is the Goal

A woman in the 56–60 age group, who has been married twice, has had disappointments, but she is not throwing in the towel. She wrote, "Many men are too needy and impatient. Older ones are arrogant. But, I am not giving up—younger men validate us and make us feel special. I just experienced one of the most wonderful long weekends of my life with a gentleman twelve years younger with whom I've developed a long-distance friendship. Surely hoping for a repeat; if not, I'll treasure the memories."

A twice-married woman in the 50–55 age group wrote that she hadn't dated since her divorce and decided to attend a singles dance. She met _____. "He is such an unforgettable character, I felt such passion and joy and love. I danced all night and I never wanted it to end… I know we are not going to marry, but God loves sinners. …My life has just started. I know that life is wonderful."

Another twice-married women in the 56–60 age group wrote about her most romantic story. "A military man—tall, dark, handsome paratrooper for New Years Eve in North Carolina. There was a romantic dinner following a party. Mink blanket on the floor, champagne, huge fresh whole strawberries, bubble bath with candlelight, three delightful days of this followed—great memory!"

A man in the 56–60 age category who had been married twice wrote about a romantic coincidence. He "made a connection through an on-line dating service… She said she went to a local high school—same one I went to. I asked her maiden name and recognized it because I dated her sister once. My name had also changed, so she didn't know me either!"

Intimidating

A twice-married gentleman in the 61–65 age group had met a woman on-line, talked on the phone, and met for dinner. "When dinner was over, I asked to excuse myself for a moment. She said, 'Where do you think you are going?' 'To the bathroom.' I said. 'Well, you better come back. The last guy that said that just left and left me with the bill.' I took out my credit card and put it on the table. I told her what Arnold would say, 'I'll be back.'"

Risky

A woman in the 66–70 age group who has been single for thirty years shared this surprising story. "Someone who was a blind date and sounded great on the phone met me in a restaurant. I was very interested until he excused himself, went to the bathroom, and came out dressed as a woman. Yikes! He said he wanted to be honest and see my reaction to a cross dresser!"

A currently single gentleman in the 61–65 age group had the following adventure between his two marriages. While using a dating service, he was picked by this very attractive lady in her early fifties. "She seemed perfect for me. We had similar interests, and she would do anything to make sure I was happy. After two months of heavy dating, I found out that she was losing her home, so I let her move into my lake home (first mistake). We traveled to the Caribbean and made love on the beach, etc. I thought that I had died and gone to heaven. Then reality set in. First clue was she told me she had been married two times when it was really five. One Friday night after working all week, I walk into my home expecting a great weekend of fun and romance, and there sits her, her mother, and two grown-up children who were in their twenties. They said they were hungry and asked what's for supper. Later that evening, she and I had a serious talk. I said I'm not providing for three generations of her family, and I think that the honeymoon is over. I moved her out, paid for three-month storage, found her an apartment. She later stalked me, caused major damage to several cars of new girlfriends, and kept a key, which she later used to destroy my TV and stereo equipment. I got a restraining order on her, and it finally ended."

Time

A woman in the 50–55 age group, who has been married once, wrote about wasting years of time. "I put three years into a relationship. He was worried about wasting his time. We broke up at Thanksgiving. We saw each other a few times in the next two months, so I believed we had a chance to get back together again. Three months after Thanksgiving, he tells me we are not compatible. I found out from his brother that he was engaged to another woman three months after Thanksgiving. He was married five months after our breakup at Thanksgiving. I was the one who wasted three years in that relationship! Disgusting!"

Expensive

"A gentleman asked me out to dinner, and we planned to meet at a nice local restaurant. I arrived early, then ordered, and paid for a bottle of wine for our dinner, because I thought it would be perceived as a nice gesture. When my date arrived, I offered him a glass of wine only to be told he didn't drink. Okay, that wasn't a problem. We ordered our dinners and had a nice conversation while we ate. When we were finished eating, the waitress placed the bill in the middle of the table. Our conversation continued, and my date didn't pick up the bill. The evening continued, and he still didn't pick up the bill. Remember now, he had asked me out for dinner. He finally suggested that we split the check. I found this to be ridiculous, and to give him a hint, I said, 'Oh, that's silly. I'll pay the bill.' And I did just that. I was actually stupid enough to go out with him again! I have since met two other women he has taken out to dinner. and he pulled the same check-splitting move on them."

Disappointing

A man in the 61–65 age group, who has been married once, wrote the following. "On a recent dinner date, we were having a nice conversation on a variety of topics when she asked me what my SAT score was. My reply was that I had no idea; it was so long ago that I didn't have a clue. In a very short period of time, she was getting very annoyed that I didn't know the answer to such a simple question. Her glass of wine may have prompted this behavior and her true self was emerging; I don't know. After what seemed like an eternity through her inquisition, we finally left the restaurant and parted company; we drove separately. On the way home, I thought I would never hear from her again, nor did I want to. The next day, she called me to tell me what a wonderful time she had and looked forward to doing it again sometime. I thought to myself, *I would rather have a root canal than go through another ordeal like that.*"

A woman who has been married twice and is in the 66–70 age category said, "I had just one date with a man who was cheap, bossed me around telling me where to set my thermostat, and smelled of garlic. And that was before we ate Italian food!"

A woman in the 66–70 year category seems to be experiencing disappointment in many ways. "Men want to have sex, but can't perform (even with pills); therefore, it becomes a very uncomfortable situation. Some men want to always be around you and many women are quite independent. They like to do things with other ladies and their families. It seems like men are more needy."

Reflections on Chapter Five

- Both younger and older LaterDaters™ surveyed associated dating with the term fun more often than negative terms including intimidating, risky, expensive, and time consuming.

- Don't hide behind your dating fears. Information is power and there are lots of other LaterDaters™ out there who are finding dating fun. You can too.

- Our dating experiences vary and most likely impact our perceptions of dating, but at the same time, they don't have to keep us from meeting new people and seeking new experiences.

CHAPTER SIX
♥

> I think I could do better than this guy.

> She's great but there are so many more to meet.

> By the time a person finds greener pastures they may be too old to climb the fence.

What Qualities are You Seeking?

What Qualities are You Seeking in That Special Person?

If you had one minute, and a pencil and paper, to jot down the qualities you would like your next sweetie to possess, what would you write? How fast would that pencil move? Would the adjectives almost gush onto the paper? Maybe we should talk.

Lonely writes:

I am sixty-two years old, and my husband died two years ago. He was the greatest guy in the world and my best friend. We met in college and were married for almost forty years. Our adult children are doing all they can to make sure that Mom is ok, but to tell the truth, I'm not. The house seems empty, and now that I am retired, I find that some days have too many hours. My lady friends have been a blessing because they include me in their activities—but not the couples events. I've dated six different men, but none of them interested me. One guy was a smoker, another used incorrect English, and one of them didn't even offer to pay for my coffee. Where have all the gentlemen gone? Would a new romance cure my loneliness?

Dear Lonely:

I am sorry your husband is no longer sharing your life, and I clearly understand that you may compare anyone you date with him. Don't miss out on the companionship you want by requiring a new sweetheart to be a carbon copy of your late husband. Use chapter six to describe a new man that you might enjoy dating. Try to focus on the good qualities in the people you date, and remember that romances usually don't knock on your door. Not every person you meet for coffee will have all the qualities you desire, but enjoy learning about another person and learn a little bit more about yourself each time.

Good luck, Linda

Please get out a pen or pencil and fill in the following checklist. It is important to understand the qualities you are looking for in a date. If you have an urge to add more words to the list, be my guest.

Which qualities are you seeking in a mate? (check all that apply)

- ☐ Similar Interests
- ☐ Healthy Lifestyle
- ☐ Similar Religious Beliefs
- ☐ Similar Political Beliefs
- ☐ Physically Attractive
- ☐ Kindhearted
- ☐ Intelligent
- ☐ Financially Secure
- ☐ Witty/Humorous
- ☐ Social/Outgoing
- ☐ Similar in Age
- ☐ Sensual/Sexually Active
- ☐ Other

I don't know which boxes you checked, but if you are like most of the people who returned the survey, you may have checked many or all of them. Many of the people who took the survey added lots of additional desired qualities in the white space on the right side of the survey page. Let's just say that many of us want someone who could walk on water.

Because we are over the age of fifty, we have likely had the opportunity to participate in more than two or three romantic relationships in our lifetime, and consequently, we have a longer list of qualities we want in a sweetheart. Our definition of Mr. or Ms. Right becomes more complex with time. If you think back to your high school dating qualifiers, you probably had a short list. For teenage boys, the list was "cute, cute, and puts out," and for the fussy teenage girl it was "cute, cute, and car."

Mr. or Ms. Wonderful was still fairly easy to find at twenty-five. He or she was attractive, nice to you, had a similar education and religious background, and your friends and family liked that person. The list of qualities you sought was shorter. You dated, maybe moved in together, and probably got married.

Fast forward thirty, forty, or fifty years and you are not married, probably a parent, looking for good care for your elderly parents, and saving for or enjoying retirement. During those years, you've had thousands of experiences that have made you more aware and discriminating than you were at sixteen or twenty-five. You may have developed a stronger religious belief or dropped religion from your life altogether. You probably have chosen a political philosophy, and have fairly strong opinions on a number of topics; you have achieved success in your work, or you may owe lots of people lots of money. You have maintained a healthy lifestyle, or you have become best friends with the Barcalounger. Maybe you've traveled the world, or maybe you haven't left the state.

In other words, you are a much more complex person at your current age than you could have imagined when you were twenty-five. Your definition of Mr. or Ms. Wonderful has become more complex too. The short list of things you were looking for in a mate at twenty-five has turned into a lengthy list of things you want and those that you will not tolerate.

We have often heard, "With age comes wisdom," but wise or not, many of us now have a very long and refined list of qualities that we desire in a date or a mate. The ultimate list can be seen on eHarmony. On this web site, you get to choose five from a very long list of positive and negative human traits. When I first used this service in 2005, the site informed me that, based on the combination of traits I selected, there wasn't one single eHarmony sweetheart for me in the entire country! This, I will admit, was a little disheartening. When I tried again in 2007, there were at least fifteen men in the St. Paul/Minneapolis metropolitan area that I could contact. A male friend of mine had the same sad fate back in 2005, only to see his options improve as the site grew. A sixty-year-old woman, who has been emailing me her dating experiences, used eHarmony and was handed one name of a seventy-five-year-old man in another state as her only perfect match. As membership grows in any on-line service, so do your chances of finding some wonderful people to date. We LaterDaters™ are hard to match up because we are seeking so many more qualities in a sweetheart than younger daters.

Interestingly, just about the only quality never mentioned on the returned surveys was "He/she would make cute babies." As we all know, men and women date for a wide variety of reasons. They are seeking certain qualities in that person who could become their life partner, but at our age, almost no one is planning to start or add to their family. At the same time, sensual or sexual was a quality selected by many of the people who responded to the survey. Biology tells us that mating is for reproduction, but it certainly serves other purposes as well. When we were young we were scared to death that fooling around would result in pregnancy; many of us married and fooled around to create a family, and now we get to fool around for fun. Don't disgust your children with this information because they want to believe that their parents are just around to help with the grandchildren, play some golf or bridge, and maybe take a cruise or two. We may be biologically useless to our species, but we're still looking for companionship, romance, love, sex, and maybe even marriage. The truth is that most of us are savvy about sex, but are dullards when it comes to dating.

In this chapter we'll see what qualities two hundred single men and women over the age of fifty are looking for in the people they date.

In analyzing the chart on page 45, we can see that there are many qualities that both sexes seem to desire in one another. Similar interests topped the charts for both men (85 percent) and women (88 percent). The following qualities also received high responses: healthy lifestyle (73 percent and 78 percent), kindhearted (73 percent and 86 percent), intelligent (72 percent and 87 percent). Similar religious or

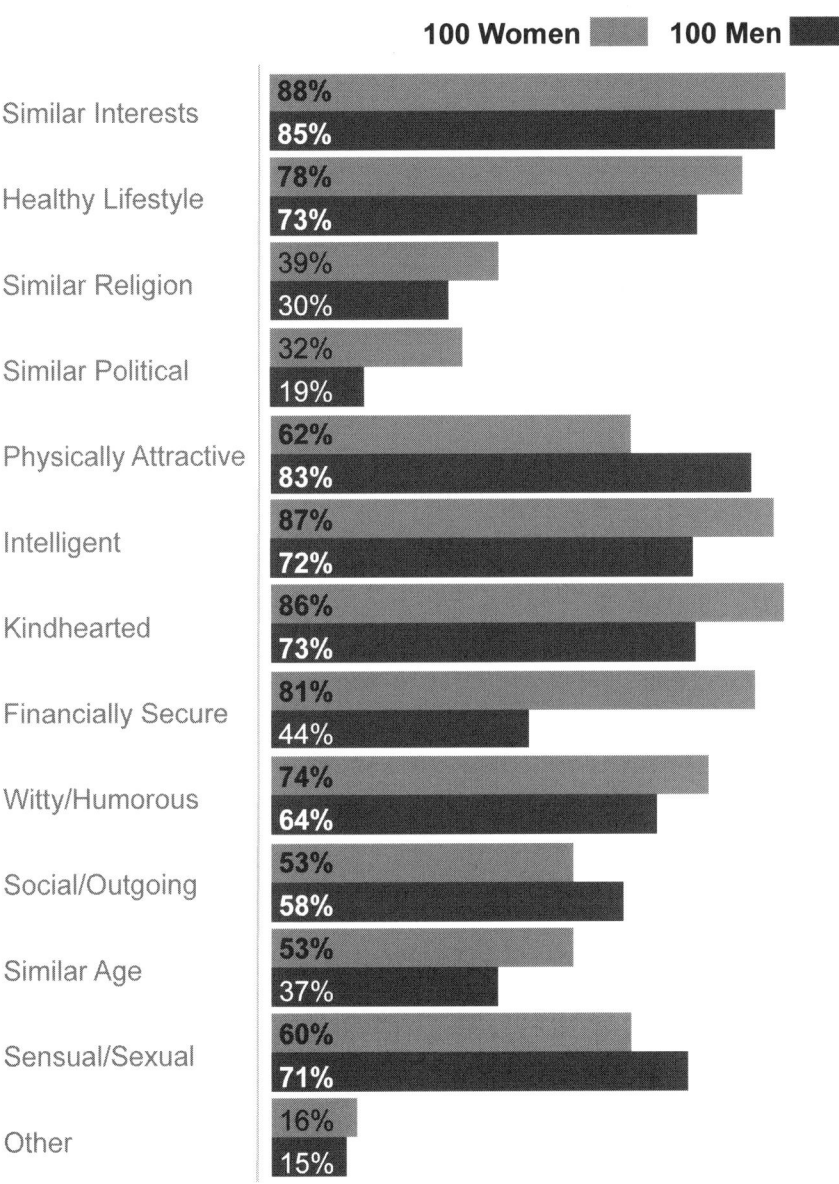

TABLE 6.1: QUALITIES FEMALES AND MALES ARE SEEKING IN A DATE

100 Women / 100 Men

Quality	100 Women	100 Men
Similar Interests	88%	85%
Healthy Lifestyle	78%	73%
Similar Religion	39%	30%
Similar Political	32%	19%
Physically Attractive	62%	83%
Intelligent	87%	72%
Kindhearted	86%	73%
Financially Secure	81%	44%
Witty/Humorous	74%	64%
Social/Outgoing	53%	58%
Similar Age	53%	37%
Sensual/Sexual	60%	71%
Other	16%	15%

Respondents chose more than one quality.

political beliefs did not appear to be as important. Approximately half of the participants listed the social and outgoing trait as something they are seeking. Apparently women chose wit more often than sex (74 percent to 60 percent) and men chose sex over wit (71 percent to 64 percent). I thought we all agree that you need a sense of humor to really enjoy sex.

For women who accuse men of being interested in women's physical qualities, and for men who accuse women of being interested in men's bank accounts, the survey findings reflect those generalities. Eight-three percent of men indicated that they desired someone who was physically attractive, while 81 percent of women checked financially secure. But, clearly, some of the other qualities discussed above are equally, if not more important, including similar interests, intelligence, and kind hearted.

Similarity in age was important to 53 percent of the women and 37 percent of the men. Don't jump to conclusions about which gender is seeking younger or older mates. An article in *AARP: the Magazine* (Nov–Dec 2005, page 44) found that "one third of older single women who are dating have a younger partner." In addition, the widely accepted belief that men over fifty want to date much younger woman turns out to be less than true. Women usually only see the first years of a man's single status behavior–"the child in a candy store" phase. This phase happens when a widower or divorced or never-married man is first back in circulation. As time passes, he notices that his children do not see this person as an acceptable stepmother and that the younger woman has none of the historical references and life experiences that he has. This leads to very limited conversations. Interviews with men from sixty to ninety-three indicated men most often wind up with women somewhere close to their own age. A few men stick with the younger women, but the majority gravitate toward someone closer to their own generational group (Gross 2000).

I think that if LaterDaters™ were awakened in the middle of the night and asked what they want in a sweetheart, they would say what one of the survey respondents wrote, "Someone who has a joyful energy. They don't have to be physically perfect or wealthy, but we need to share some of the same interests so that we can be companions on this trip called life." I think this last statement sums up the survey results.

None of the qualities should be seen as insurmountable obstacles to dating fun, but instead as information from and about other LaterDaters™. Eighty-three percent of the men indicated physically attractive as a quality they are seeking, but they didn't cross that out and write in drop dead gorgeous. Women chose a triumvirate of intelligent/kindhearted/financially secure. They didn't cross that out and write in brilliant/philanthropic/billionaire.

Did your choices align with the two hundred women and men who took the survey? Are you looking for more, less, or different qualities? Do you think that we seek different qualities in people as we grow older? Let's look at the next table (page 48) to answer that question.

The five qualities that seem important for people in all age groups are similar interests, healthy lifestyle, kindhearted, intelligent, and physically attractive. Similar religious and political beliefs were less important across all of the age groups. The importance of finding a sweetheart who is social/outgoing seems to fluctuate a little between age groups, as does the importance of similarity in age. Seeking a mate who is sensual/sexually active appears to become less important with age. This doesn't seem like a big surprise, but what's interesting to me is that only 71 percent of the survey respondents between 50 and 55 checked this quality. If you are in that age group (50–55) and didn't check sensual/sexually active, be sure to read chapter thirteen, "Better Living Through Chemistry."

Of the eight people over the age of seventy-five who completed the survey, 31 percent (three) of them chose sensual/sexually active as a quality they were seeking in a mate. Author Margaret Roden studied sixty dating people over the age of sixty in her paper "Love and Romance over the Life Cycle." She concluded, "While intimacy needs were still important, the definitions of love take on a more pragmatic and companionate [sic] aspects as one ages." This is supported in our data by noting that the percentages of people choosing similar interests remains high in all age groups.

Most of us are looking for much more than we did when we were younger, but it doesn't appear that we all want it all. There certainly were survey respondents that marked every single quality and then added to the list lots of other qualities such as doesn't gamble or drink (see the other column). But seem to share more in terms of what

TABLE 6.2 QUALITIES SOUGHT COMPARED BY AGE GROUPS

Ages ▶ Perceptions ▼	50-55 N=45	56-60 N=60	61-65 N=47	66-70 N=30	71-75 N=15	75 + N=8
Similar Interests	**91%**	**89%**	**91%**	**80%**	**69%**	**63%**
Healthy Lifestyle	**82%**	**81%**	**66%**	**77%**	**69%**	**63%**
Similar Religion	**59%**	33%	26%	27%	23%	13%
Similar Politically	27%	23%	30%	27%	31%	0%
Physically Attractive	**80%**	**70%**	**74%**	**70%**	**62%**	**63%**
Kind-hearted	**78%**	**81%**	**81%**	**83%**	**77%**	**63%**
Intelligent	**76%**	**84%**	**89%**	**63%**	**77%**	**75%**
Financially Secure	**73%**	**65%**	**55%**	**57%**	**62%**	50%
Witty/ Humorous	**69%**	**75%**	**72%**	**63%**	**62%**	38%
Social/ Outgoing	42%	**58%**	**60%**	**67%**	46%	**63%**
Similar in Age	40%	47%	45%	**53%**	46%	25%
Sensual/ Sexual	**71%**	**72%**	**68%**	**57%**	46%	31%
Other	20%	18%	13%	10%	8%	25%

N = number of respondents in each age group.
Respondents chose more than one quality.
Bold numbers indicate qualities selected by more than 50%.

we are looking for than not. Maybe this LaterDating™ thing isn't an impossible feat.

Once, on a date at a coffee shop, the man I was with summarized the problem of adult dating by using the analogy of a five-hundred-piece puzzle. Both people come to the date looking for lots of qualities in the other person. The list of qualities is so long that the chance of two people finding them all in one human being is unlikely. His solution was to just let some of those pieces "drop to the floor." Decide what is of primary importance to the big picture and forget the rest.

I learned a lot about myself from that coffee date. He was complimentary to me during this date, but he was also honest and observant. He said he thought I was probably a rigid person. I've always admitted to being a type A, but rigid threw me. After thinking about this for a day (I'm a little slow), I realized he was correct—I have trouble letting any puzzle pieces drop to the floor. I had searched for every possible defect in my future Mr. Wonderful. *The only defects I hadn't seen were my own.* I began the search then and there.

Do we learn from the mistakes made in past relationships? Do we become more or less accepting of defects in partners? Do we demand more or less from future relationships? The next section should help answer these questions.

Those people in the survey who had never been married generally sought fewer qualities (with the exception of similar age) when compared with those who had been married once, twice, or more. Could this be that old truism: "Fool me once, shame on you; fool me twice, shame on me"? Does divorce make us more aware of relationship pitfalls and make us more demanding in our future dating choices? Please note that the number of respondents who have been married three times or more was very low (four).

It is notable that people surveyed who had never been married had the shortest list of qualities sought. The people with the longest wish list had been married once or more. It might be helpful to reflect on your own list of qualities and your past experiences. Are you working on a puzzle with five hundred pieces, and if so, are you willing to drop any of them?

TABLE 6.3 TIMES MARRIED MAY AFFECT THE QUALITIES WE SEEK

Times Married ▶ Qualities ▼	0 Times N=30	1 Time N=123	2 Times N=43	3 Times N=4
Similar Interests	**80%**	**90%**	**79%**	**100%**
Healthy Lifestyle	**57%**	**81%**	**70%**	**100%**
Similar Religion	33%	38%	23%	**50%**
Similar Politically	20%	28%	21%	25%
Physically Attractive	**67%**	**71%**	**81%**	**75%**
Kind-hearted	**57%**	**85%**	**81%**	**75%**
Intelligent	**73%**	**81%**	**79%**	**100%**
Financially Secure	37%	**69%**	**63%**	**50%**
Witty/ Humorous	**57%**	**73%**	**65%**	**75%**
Social/ Outgoing	47%	**61%**	44%	**75%**
Similar Age	**50%**	46%	35%	**75%**
Sensual/ Sexual	**63%**	**67%**	**63%**	**75%**
Other	23%	13%	19%	0%

N = number of respondents.
Respondents chose more than one quality.
Numbers in bold indicate qualities selected by more than 50%.

CHAPTER SIX ♥ 51

Your Stories

The stories poured in about qualities that were sought and about the disasters that can occur when they are not present in your date or in yourself. Remember that all of the people in these stories had chosen to go out with one another. At first, they probably saw some of the positive qualities they were looking for in a sweetheart, but then they saw another side of that person.

Similar Interests

People who have similar interests are logically attracted to one another. The next story came from a man in the 56–60 age group. "We were at a nice restaurant, enjoying the food and each other. We were still getting acquainted. She asked, 'Do you watch much TV?' When I said, 'I don't have one,' she blurted out, 'Will you marry me?' And then she laughed right away—she had surprised herself with that one. So she explained that her former husband was a television addict, and she wanted to avoid repeating that."

Another woman in the 66–70 age group wrote that she hasn't dated for three years because she "hurt a few people by having to say she wasn't interested in them romantically after many months of dating." Was this woman looking for companionship, but not intimacy? There are gentlemen who have similar interests.

Another survey respondent described "Attempting to communicate with a Serbian women with limited English and me with virtually no Serbian language skills." As I hear about more and more people seeking mates from other countries, I can't help but think about how hard it is to communicate when two people share the same native language! Similar interests would be essential.

Healthy Lifestyle

"Dating someone who turns out to be a gambling addict is terrible. It isn't something you can detect until you are into the relationship." A relationship with a gambling addict could cost you much more than the temporary hurt of a breakup.

Similar Religion

The next contributor was in the 66–70 age group and she had created some rules for dating men over sixty. He must be "compatible, conscientious, communicable [sic], caring, and a Christian." He must not be "a controller, conceited, contemptuous, a criticizer, or a cranky creep."

Similar Politically

No one wrote to me about political incompatibility, and the survey results show that most people don't care. I have noticed, however, that women tend to become more liberal as they get older and men tend to become more conservative. Quite a few men have expressed their disapproval of my political leanings, and I never hear from them again.

Physically Attractive

This next story questions a man's right to be vain. The couple was driving home after a nice dinner when she noticed that his black hair was gray around the edges. He was wearing a very bad toupee. She didn't want to date a man who wore a wig, but she wouldn't have minded dating a bald man. "Why are men so vain?" she asked. The answer is that we are all somewhat vain, and thank goodness we are that way. Perhaps vanity pushes us to keep ourselves clean, in-shape, and well groomed. By the way, I, too, am one of the millions of women who really like bald men and dislike toupees.

"I'm not ugly. But I'm not beautiful either. The world favors beautiful, good-looking people. Looks are important to me too. It's just that I wish people (men) were more willing to get involved with someone who is average looking. I have a big heart and lots to give."

This person readily admits that looks are important to her too. I would like to ask her if there was one thing she could physically change about herself, what would it be? Is the change do-able? Certainly a new hairstyle, a make-up make over or some clothing consultation is not out of the question for most women. Diet and exercise require dedication, but the results are rewarding. For those people who are able to afford plastic surgery, be aware that plastic surgeons get seven years of training after medical school and cosmetic surgeons get one year of training after medical school. If you should choose plastic surgery, don't ever do something so serious on the cheap. Please research the doctor before you hire him or her to change your body or your face. Doctors who are not certified dermatologists can legally do chemical peels, use lasers, and inject Botox and facial fillers such as Restalyn. I think it is a smarter to find a cosmetic dermatologist to do these procedures. Again, do your research—better safe than sorry. And remember that physically attractive was not the most highly selected quality.

"I joined a dating service and most of the men wanted slim women (which I'm not) and they were fatter than pigs." The survey charts in this chapter certainly do confirm that men place physically attractive close to the top of their desired qualities in a woman. Maybe they can't help themselves. In my opinion, males are biologically programmed to attempt to mate with healthy females. In our culture, healthy tends to mean slim, and many men look for it.

Another gentleman in the 61–65 age group "met a lady at a dance. She had long blonde hair and we made a date for the next week. When I picked her up, I could hardly believe my eyes. She had chopped off her hair, had a tight perm, and dyed it reddish brown. She did not look good at all! We were going out for dinner and she had on white tennis shoes. So, never judge a girl by one meeting!" I sometimes wonder what would happen if all the women in the world had long blond extensions added to their hair. This seems to be such a universal turn-on to men that I would sadly predict a soaring birthrate among the younger set and a big increase in car accidents by men over the age of fifty.

Kindhearted

A gentleman in the 66–70 age group wishes that women would be more kindhearted. "Women after fifty seem to fall into three distinct classifications. 1. They have never been married and there just isn't room in her life to fit another person; therefore, you are no more than an object to get her friends to leave her alone. 2. Their husbands left them for another, and therefore, all men are obviously no good rotten animals that aren't to be trusted. 3. The poor guy died, but the good news is he became a saint and no man on the planet can live up to her expectations. I don't mean to be cruel, but please, ladies, have a heart, and try to meet men for who they are as individuals and what they have to offer. You may be surprised; some of us do not drag our knuckles when we walk." Well said.

Intelligent

"Last year I started dating a newly divorced man—what a disaster! Let's just call him The Putz. We would go out to dinner several times a week. We went to the casino and shared a hotel room. I made the mistake of having sex with him. It was simply the worst time of my life. The worst part of the story is that I kept seeing him, simply out of loneliness. Then he dumped me. Talk about depressing. I was dumped by The Putz!"

Financially Secure

If you're a woman, read the following story. "My financial advisor set me up for a date with his golf buddy, and when he came to pick me up, he had an old wrecker of a car, and I told my daughter to tell him I wasn't feeling well. She made me go. She said, 'you always told us we had to go if we said we would.'" It's possible that women are biologically programmed to attempt to mate with strong males. In our culture, to many women, strong means financially secure.

Witty/Humorous

The tables in chapter six indicate that being witty and humorous are qualities that many people seek in someone to date—but no one included a story about it. My own experiences have taught me to tune my humor to the level of my date's humor. This doesn't mean I have to revert to knock-knock jokes, but in my dating experience many men don't like to be outwitted.

Social/Outgoing

A woman in the 61–65 age group, who had been married once, agreed to go on a sailing trip with someone she had been enjoying dating. Many of us can probably relate to her story of "seeing him in a very different light when he was with his friends—and then feeling trapped!" Spending time with someone on a date usually allows two people to focus on one another. Group settings reveal how we behave in a wider social situation.

Similar Age

That age thing is creeping up on all of us. Does it negatively affect women more than men? A gentleman in the 61–65 age category contacted a woman through an on-line dating service. "Beautiful, long blond hair, tall, slim, great figure, no wrinkles, and looked like she was about forty years old. She said in her profile that she was sixty years old (two years younger than me) and widowed. She owned a Harley, a sports car, an SUV, a nice house, and was full of energy and fun. On top of that, she was a great cook. This has some possibilities! We dated a number of times and really hit it off. She started talking like we should have a committed relationship. I was interested. Uh-oh, this is getting serious. Then one night after a great dinner at her house, she dropped the bomb—with a guilty look she says she had lied about her age. OK, I thought, so she's a young chick—maybe I can deal with that. Might even be fun. My mind is racing—do I really want a young chick, have I struck gold? What are my kids going to think about me dating someone their age? Then she told me she was seventy-two years old. Ah, the wonders of modern medicine and plastic surgery." This story illustrates what it seems that men want: they want someone who looks young, but is close to their own age.

A man in the 66–70 age group contributed this odd story about dating and age. "A few years after I was divorced, I got to know a young lady who was a few years younger than me. To make a long story short, I started dating this young lady's mother. I would take the mother out on a date—then, a few days later, I would take the daughter out on a date, and I was getting tired." A hearty fellow, indeed.

Sensual/Sexual

It is only logical that this quality becomes less important as we age, and it is also logical that no one wanted to share a story about this very personal part of their life.

Other

I often hear the word chemistry mentioned when I talk to other LaterDaters™ about the dating and mating scene. You will notice that chemistry was not listed on the charts about the qualities people are seeking. The world of chemistry in dating is impossible to explain because it involves different elements for different people. A personality that you find pleasing, stirred together with a physical presence that you find attractive, could be a recipe for good chemistry. Because each of us is deciding on what is pleasing and what is attractive, this chemical formula is going to be different for each of us.

The following fictional story tells about one man's definition of chemistry.

A man wanted to get married. He was having trouble choosing among three likely candidates. He gave each woman a present of $5,000. He watched to see what each one did with the money.

The first had a total make over. She went to a fancy beauty salon got her hair done, new make-up, bought several new outfits, and dressed up very nicely for her man. She told him that she did this to be more attractive for him because she loved him so much. The man was impressed.

The second went shopping to buy the man gifts. She got him a new set of golf clubs, some new gizmos for his computer, and some expensive clothes. As she presented these gifts, she told him that she spent all the money on him because she loved him so much. Again, the man is impressed.

The third invested the money in the stock market. She earned several times the $5,000. She gave him back his $5,000 and reinvested the remainder in a joint account. She told him that she wanted to save for their future because she loved him so much. Obviously, the man was impressed.

The man thought for a long time about what each woman had done with the money he'd given her. Then he married the one with the biggest boobs. It's always hard to predict the qualities another person will choose.

Reflections on Chapter Six

- Similar interests are important to us LaterDaters™

- The older age groups of the LaterDaters™ surveyed sought fewer qualities than the younger groups. Maybe we do get wiser with age.

- People who had never been married had the shortest lists of qualities they are seeking in a sweetheart, while those of us who had been married have the longer lists.

- It's important to keep our lists in check.

CHAPTER SEVEN

♥

> No wonder the dating service didn't show me his photo.

> The dating service owes me a refund on this one.

> The cheapest face-lift is a smile.

What are the Most Effective Methods for Meeting People to Date?

Of all the questions LaterDaters™ have about dating, the question that is the title of this chapter is probably the most important. We all have our comfort zones. Many of us feel out of place in bars, where most of the clientele is younger—and we may run into our children there. The workplace is full of younger people too, and most of us do not want to look like old fools in an office romance. The Internet has become a haven for many LaterDaters™ because we can shop on-line for someone to meet and possibly date. This method works for some, but many of us want more options in the search of a sweetie.

Where Do I Start writes:

I would love to have a special person in my life, but my life is such a mess I can't imagine who would want me. I'm fifty-two and recently divorced for the second time. I was such a zombie from the divorce that I was fired from my job. My finances are a mess. I can't afford a computer for on-line dating and those lunch or dinner singles groups would be over my budget. Frankly, I need a man in my life not only for companionship, but also for some financial stability. My friends and family seem to think

I should be able to find someone because I'm not overweight, have a good sense of humor, and love to dance. Maybe there is someone out there for me, but where do I start looking?

Dear Where:

You just described two problems. The employment issue needs to be solved first because it will positively impact your finances, your self-esteem, and your datability. Secondly, go to the library and use a computer to look up two things: free on-line dating and locating singles dances. Meetup.com would be a good starting point for finding those dances. The information in chapter seven will give you more ideas for finding that someone you are seeking. Oh, and please fill out the form after this letter.

Thanks, and good luck, Linda

What methods have you tried and what methods have you found effective? (check all that apply)

Methods	Tried	Found Effective
Through Friends/Relatives		
Hanging Out (in bars or coffee shops)		
Joining Activities (i.e., sports, dancing, cooking)		
Attending Singles Dances		
Using On-line Dating Sites		
Participating In Speed Dating Events		
Using Dating Services (off-line)		
Using Personal Ads (in newspapers and magazines)		
Taking Singles Vacations		
Joining Interest Groups (i.e., book, church groups)		
Other (List)		
Other (List)		

CHAPTER SEVEN

What methods have you used to meet a sweetheart, and which of them did you find effective? Dear reader, check all that apply. Don't skip this simple exercise because it will be helpful to you in determining your future dating strategies.

Hopefully, you have tried some or many of the options listed and at least some of them have produced some dating opportunities. If you are staring at a blank chart, you need to ask yourself a hard question. Do you think that the FedEx man or woman is going to come to your door and fall in love with you? This chapter could be titled "Try, Try, and Try Again," because, for the majority of us, this is what it takes to meet the right person. For those of you who are saying, "Oh well, if it is meant to be, I will meet him or her," let me remind you that astrology is not a science. Market research is necessary to find a good car, a good TV, and a good sweetheart. You will need to leave the security of your kitchen or couch and venture out into the world of people. Most people want to have a wonderful relationship just as you do, so you should think of them as future friends, not the enemy.

If you live in a major metropolitan area, you can search on-line and find most of the methods listed on the chart. You will be surprised by the number of options that are available for you to meet other singles in your age group. Get help from a computer-literate friend if you must, and if you don't own a computer, go to the library.

If you live in a rural area your options are more limited. You may not have access to speed-dating events, dating services, and some activity-related groups such as cooking clubs or sports clubs. What's happening in the nearest large town? Use that town's name in your computer search, and you may find that all of those services and clubs unavailable in your small town are happening right down the highway.

What Methods Have Been Tried and Worked for Others?

The following chart reveals how two hundred women and men responded to the question: What methods have you used to meet a sweetheart, and which of them did you find effective? The majority of the survey respondents had tried many different ways to meet others. What did they find to be most effective? Let's find out.

TABLE 7.1: DATING METHODS TRIED AND FOUND EFFECTIVE BY GENDER

Methods	No. Tried	Number of Women Successful / Number of Men Successful
Friends & Relatives	60 / 62	18 / 27
Bars & Coffee	30 / 36	6 / 10
Joining Activities	55 / 64	30 / 50
Singles Dances	57 / 54	21 / 37
On-line Dating	37 / 44	13 / 24
Speed Dating	19 / 21	3 / 7
Dating Services	16 / 17	3 / 8
Personal Ads	24 / 27	7 / 14
Singles Vacations	7 / 9	1 / 4
Interest Groups	37 / 38	14 / 23
Other	14 / 9	6 / 3

Respondents chose more than one method.

What should men and women do to find a date? The numbers that jump out at me in this chart are the ones showing that every method of meeting a sweetheart is reported to be more effective by the men than by the women (with the exception of the "Other" category). That "Other" category was most often defined as the workplace. There may be two reasons for this phenomenon. One, men usually assume the traditional role of the pursuer in a social setting, so they have the advantage of starting a conversation without appearing aggressive. Two, the census data show that there are more single women over the age of fifty than there are single men. This statistic also helps explain men's greater success on the dating scene.

So what's a girl to do? Check the numbers. Women are experiencing a 55 percent success rate for finding dates in singles groups that are formed around activities. This could include golf, tennis, skiing, biking, hiking, dancing, bridge, or any other activity that you enjoy. It's not coincidental that men are also having their best luck (78 percent) in groups that are organized around an activity. Meetup.com is a nationwide source for activity groups. It makes sense that people who share an interest in the same activity may find it easier to talk to one another and possibly enjoy one another's company.

There were other methods that were reported to be effective for both men and women; interest groups, on-line dating, and singles dances. Interest groups include things like book clubs, cooking classes, and the most frequently mentioned—religious organizations. It is important to remember that you should join these interest groups only if you have an actual interest in the topic; just having an interest in the opposite sex is probably not going to serve you well in this venue. Another method that deserves attention is on-line dating. Women reported a 35 percent approval rating (thirteen found it effective out of thirty-seven tries). On-line dating is an efficient way for shy people to begin a conversation and possibly agree to meet for coffee or a drink. If you live in a small town, it allows you to find singles in areas close to you, or even in other states or countries. Singles dances are also one of the more effective methods of finding someone to date. You will be enjoying a party atmosphere, getting some exercise, and possibly finding a sweetie.

There are a few methods on the table that indicate strategies with lower success rates particularly for women respondents. Dating services proved successful for only eleven people out of the thirty-three who paid for them. Half of the men and only 18 percent of the women were happy with this method. Dating services can be expensive, so buyer beware. Bars and coffee shops proved less effective (worked for 20 percent of the women who tried and 27 percent of the men), as did speed dating (worked for 16 percent of the women who tried and 33 percent of the men). I think both speed dating and bars/coffee houses are great places to meet people if you are an extroverted person who enjoys striking up conversations with people you haven't met before. Of the seven women in our survey who had tried a singles vacation, only one found a future date there. Almost half of the nine men who went on singles vacations said they were a good way to meet women. Personal ads worked for half of the men who used them, but only for seven out of the twenty-four women who did.

The first method shown on the chart, friends/relatives, indicated that lots of people thought this would be an excellent way to meet someone to date. Sixty women and sixty-two men out of a total of two hundred survey respondents have attempted this method. Only eighteen of the sixty women managed to find matches with the help of friends and relatives. The sixty-two men fared better with their friends and relatives finding suitable women for them to date in twenty-seven cases. Apparently friends and relatives are willing to help us out in our search for someone to date, but they don't always get it right.

There are lots of things to try, but beyond gender differences, what works best for whom? When the data was disaggregatd by age, I found that there was some helpful information to assist you in finding someone to share a bag of popcorn at the movies. Find your age group on table 7.2A to find out what might work best for you in the LaterDating™ world.

What should you do, at your age, to get a date? According to the two hundred active LaterDaters™ surveyed, the most effective method for meeting someone to date across the age categories looks to be—TA DAH, once again, joining a singles group formed around an activity. It would seem that joining a singles activity group is 63 percent effective even in the seventy-five-plus age group. The numbers show us that another effective way to find a date, for all but the seventy-five-plus group, is attending singles dances. There are two other methods that have some merit, depending on your age.

TABLE 7.2A DATING METHODS FOUND EFFECTIVE BY DIFFERENT AGE GROUPS

Age Groups ▶ Methods ▼	50–55 N=45	56–60 N=57	61-65 N=47	66–70 N=30	71–75 N=13	75 + N=8
Friends & Relatives	20%	14%	28%	33%	31%	13%
Bars & Coffee	11%	11%	13%	3%	0%	0%
Joining Activities	58%	32%	32%	33%	46%	63%
Singles Dances	27%	26%	34%	23%	46%	25%
On-line Dating	22%	12%	32%	13%	8%	0%
Speed Dating	9%	4%	9%	0%	0%	0%
Dating Services	11%	4%	9%	0%	0%	0%
Personal Ads	9%	7%	19%	7%	15%	0%
Singles Vacations	4%	2%	4%	0%	0%	0%
Interest Groups	20%	25%	4%	17%	31%	38%
Other Methods	0%	9%	0%	7%	8%	13%

N = number of respondents in an age category.
Some respondents chose more than one category.
If you also want to know what % of people tried these methods, please see *Table 7.2B Dating Methods Tried by Age Groups* in the appendix.

TABLE 7.3A DATING METHODS FOUND EFFECTIVE BY TIMES MARRIED

Times Married ▶ Methods ▼	Married 0 times N=30	Married 1 time N=123	Married 2 times N=43	Married 3 times N=4
Friends & Relatives	33%	18%	28%	25%
Bars & Coffee	20%	4%	9%	25%
Joining Activities	43%	44%	28%	25%
Singles Dances	27%	28%	33%	25%
On-line Dating	3%	21%	16%	75%
Speed Dating	3%	21%	16%	0%
Dating Services	7%	4%	9%	0%
Personal Ads	0%	11%	16%	25%
Singles Vacations	7%	2%	0%	0%
Interest Groups	20%	19%	19%	0%
Other Methods	3%	6%	2%	0%

N = number of respondents.
Some respondents chose many methods.
If you also want to know what % of people tried these methods, please see *Table 7.3B Dating Methods Tried by Times Married* in the appendix.

One effective method is joining interest groups (book clubs, churches, etc.) and the second is meeting people through friends and relatives. On-line services are efficient for the 50–55 group (22 percent) and the 61–65 age group (32 percent). All of the other effective numbers on the chart are quite discouraging. These low numbers tell us to forget bars and coffee shops, speed dating, dating services, personal ads, and singles vacations if we have a limited amount of time and/or money to spend on our dating search.

The research on effective methods of finding people to date indicated some differences by age categories. Now let's see what we can learn by looking at the survey responses in terms of the number of times a person had been married. If you have never been married, or married once, twice, or more times, what might be the most effective methods for you to find someone to date? What does table 7.3A show you about effective methods to find a date?

The table gives some possible dating hints to those of you who have never married, or have been married once, or more. Survey respondents who had never been married, or have only been married once, had the best luck finding dates at singles activity clubs (sports activities were high.) For the active LaterDaters™ who had been married twice, there were three methods of meeting people that almost tied for effectiveness: friends/relatives, singles activity clubs, and singles dances. Those who had been married three or more times (only four in the survey) indicated that on-line dating works the best for them.

The people who took the survey shared their stories about how they met dates. Let's learn from more of the active LaterDaters™ out there in the dating world.

Your Stories

Meeting Dates through Friends and Relatives

A gentleman in the 66–70-year age category met a woman through a friend. I will paraphrase: She was fascinated with me, and soon, I with her. We were the same age. She was smart, sensual, and talked about getting married. After about four months, she quit having contact with me. When I reached her, she said our goals were different. Six months later, I found out she was married. This man wonders:

1. Was she going with someone else while she went with me?
2. Was she going with someone, and broke it off to go with me, and then went back?
3. Was she looking for someone else while going with me?
4. Did she accidentally meet someone financially better off than I was, and he wasn't about to lose that great sensual person?

I guess I will never know.

Here's a comment from a man in the 56–60 age group about being set up by a friend. "Blind Date: worked great for five years. Best five years of my life!"

A man over seventy-five writes: "About four years ago I was attending a rededication of a friend's marriage ceremony. After the ceremony was over, I was filing out of the church when I heard my name called. It was a friend I hadn't seen in forty-five years. As a result of hearing my name called, a second man came up to me. It was the son of a couple I knew many years ago. I asked him about his family and learned that his father had died and his mother was living locally. Later, I called the mother and invited her to dinner. As a result, we've been dating ever since."

Meeting by Joining an Activity Organization Just for Singles

A man in the 56–60 group writes: "Disaster—went on a ski trip with a lady and got dumped. Success—went on a ski trip, met a lady, together ever since."

A man in the 61–65 age group shared this story. "I connected to a fellow female tennis player recently. I would not say that sparks flew, but we both showed an interest to increase our relationship to new levels. The relationship is on hold as she has been fighting a terminal disease."

Meeting Dates On-line

Of all the stories that were sent to me, the subject of on-line dating resulted in a tsunami of responses.

A man in the 66–70 age group writes: "I have met several woman through Match.com. Three have become friends that I do movies, lunch, bike rides, concerts, etc. with. I have been puzzled when women have used old pictures. When we meet, I immediately have a feeling of distrust. One of the challenges I have found: Meet on-line, email, perhaps talk on phone, meet in person, then one or both are not interested in continuing to meet—how and when do you communicate that? When others have been direct with me, or I with them, that has been the most satisfactory."

Another man (61–65 age group) stated: "I'm 5'10, 170 pounds, and I met a woman on-line that described herself as a former high hurdler in high school and a former model at the Renaissance Festival. She stated that she was 5'8" with long legs, drove a small red Pontiac Sunbird. I realized that high school was thirty years ago, but figured a former athlete would stay in reasonable shape. Set up a meeting for coffee. The woman that emerged from the small car had to be about 270 pounds. I had told her my stats, so why she thought we would be a match is beyond me. Spent what I thought was an appropriate amount of time over coffee and left."

A woman in the 61–65 age group writes: "I met a man through Match.com. We corresponded for several weeks before meeting at Stuart Anderson's for a drink. He was a wonderful writer, and I was intrigued. He advertised himself as an 'emotionally stable, no hang-ups kind of guy.' During the course of the ninety minutes or so we spent together, I found out he had been married five times, had five children, and only two of his children had any contact with him. After he had consumed four drinks within an hour and a half, I excused myself and said I had an early morning appointment. No hang-ups? He was all hang-ups."

Another man in the 71–75 age group said: "I have found it to be a turn-off if the relationship begins based on exaggerations, old photos, mistruths about age, etc. There are important things to be learned about each other, and because of age, less time to discover. So truth is very important to me and deliberate untruth is almost fatal to a relationship going forward."

I hope you are planning to be honest in your on-line dating profile and photo. I have met many nice guys using an on-line service who have said that I was the only woman they had met using an on-line service who actually told the truth and used a current photo. Why would any woman or man want to lie for a cup of coffee? Do you really think you're going to charm the other person so that he or she overlooks the deception you presented in your profile?

On-line dating can also present problems if you choose to communicate with people who live far away. For example, a gentleman in the 61–65 group writes: " Met a gal on the Internet. Traveled from Minnesota to North Carolina for a weekend. I love art, so toured the Rodin Museum. I like the outdoors, so canoed down a river—sang a French song —turns out she had French blood. I will always remember the trip. She decided against further meetings since I did not plan on living in North Carolina or Virginia where she had plans on retiring. She is now married and contact was lost. We did email for several years after the trip."

A woman (50–55 age group) also experienced a wonderful (but short) friendship because of distance. She writes: "Met someone on-line —talked on phone a couple times (talked as he drove down to Florida). Within a couple of weeks, got invited by a girlfriend to go to Florida. Checked with him. I went down a day before I was to meet my girlfriend. He picked me up at the airport. He took me on a tour of the area, had a nice lunch, visited his boat, had a great dinner, and he got me a room. Very much a gentleman. Picked me up—brought me to my friend's the next day. We're still friends—no romance, but great time."

My advice is do not lie on your profile and do not choose someone who lives far away. I have followed that first rule, but I have not always followed the second one. I corresponded on-line with a man from Florida who flew to Minnesota (in the summer) to visit me for four days. He stayed in his own apartment, and I showed him the town, which he found about as interesting as an old dishrag. He was a man who had obviously lied about his age and his personality was s-o-o-o irritating. How irritating? I got hives and had to go to the dermatologist. Remember that there are some on-line dating sites that only do national searches; others allow you to limit the distance that is searched for likely matches. Most of my on-line dating experiences have been enjoyable, and some have led to wonderful romances.

One more story about an on-line mishap. A sixty-year-old woman writes, "My carefully crafted, deeply revealing profile was attracting very questionable types due to an innocent error. I'd repeatedly used the term 'intimacy' in appealing to Mr. Right to step up to the plate. Being female, this only meant emotional intimacy. Being male—as a good guy friend finally explained to me—this term meant, 'I WANT A LOT OF SEX!' Appalled, I rewrote my profile, but not before being deluged with emails from characters with user names like: marathonlover, tonguen, lovnleather, pussypleaser, and worse."

Attending Speed Dating Events to Meet Future Dates

Speed dating is something I really like, because I'm the gabby type, but the survey shows most people don't find it effective. Speed dating involves an equal number of men and women. The organizer of the event charges everyone to attend and cheerfully explains the procedure. Every participant is given a piece of paper for taking notes and a nametag for their first names. The women are usually seated at tables, and when a chime rings, the men move from one table to the next. The conversations last about seven minutes and then everyone meets the next person in the rotation. Everyone takes notes. At the end of the event everyone turns in the first names of the people they found interesting. The next day the organizer of the event emails or calls the people who chose one another with their phone numbers or email addresses. It is then up to the individuals to contact one another for another meeting. The following two letters support the survey results.

A man in the 71–75 age group writes: "I was thinking about that speed dating. I do not believe that is a good situation.

1. Everyone is on their best behavior (almost a group in competition).
2. Everyone is eyeing each other.
3. Everyone is up tight.
4. Everyone is basically taking a stress test (I have to get out of here)."

A woman in the 56–60 age category wrote about speed dating: "My impression was that they were a stable of over-fifty guys, which you apparently had no choice but to bring in, time after time. Some even told me they didn't have to pay because the speed dating event was so desperate to fill the slots!" The writer of this statement is referring to the situation where there are twenty women who sign up for a speed dating event, but not twenty men, so the organizer needs to call in men who have previously attended in order to even the numbers.

Singles Dances Work for Some of Us

I love singles dances because I'm an old rock 'n roller. When the band plays a great oldie, I'm on the floor with whomever is willing. Not everyone is as uninhibited as I am, however, as you will read in the following stories.

A woman in the 71–75 age group writes: "Going to my first singles dance was very frightening, I could hardly contain my composure; I wanted to cry. This is what it's like being single! The men stand on the side and eye every woman walking through."

A man in that same age group briefly wrote: "Met woman at dance —got along fine. Then she reminded me; we went out twenty years ago."

Personal Ads in Publications can Lead to Interesting Results

Personal ads are still being used as a device to find that special someone. A man in the 61–65 age group wrote: "It was a disaster in Duluth. The lady answered an ad of mine. We met at a restaurant, after which I tried every conceivable approach to maintaining a conversation with her. Nothing worked, and I wound up taking her home far earlier than expected. The awkward silence during the meal was absolutely devastating. I think I felt worse than she did. Amazingly, on the preliminary phone call setting up the date, there was no hint of any communication problems."

A woman in the 61–65 age group reported this hilarious ad adventure: "I met a man through an ad in the *Reader* who seemed too good to be true. Three months later, he put another ad in while we were going strong. A friend and I answered the ad with a fictitious name and photo. We caught him waiting for her. 'What a coup!' he said while he collected his things from my house."

Reflections on Chapter Seven

- All of the dating methods the surveyed LaterDaters™ tried were reported more effective by men than women, but there were several methods found effective by many.

- Women reported a 56 percent success rate for finding someone to date by joining activities.

- The other category was usually describes as the workplace, and 43 percent of women who reported trying this method found it to be effective.

- On-line dating and singles dances were effective for 35 percent or more of the women who tried them.

- Joining activity and interest groups was reported effective by the largest numbers of surveyed LaterDaters™.

- Surveyed LaterDaters™ who had never married or had been married once reported the best luck finding dates by joining activities. While LaterDaters™ who had been married two times were most successful at singles dances, LaterDaters™ married three times or more reported that on-line services worked best for them.

A Form for Determining Your Best Dating Strategies

Since you need to know what would be the most effective methods for finding future dates, try filling out this form for ideas.

1. As a _____(woman/man), looking at table 7.1 on page 60, I see that I should try:
   _____
   _____
   _____

2. Because I am age _____, by using table 7.2A on page 63, I would most likely be successful trying:
   _____
   _____
   _____

3. I have been married _____ (0, 1, 2, 3) times and the table 7.3A on page 64 indicates I would probably find dating success if I try:
   _____
   _____
   _____

I hope you see a pattern here that will be helpful to you when you write your dating plan in chapter fifteen.

CHAPTER EIGHT

♥

> Nice, but not my type.

> Beautiful, but after four dinners there have been zero kisses.

> A bachelor wishes he had as much fun as his married friends imagine he has.

What Kind of Relationships are LaterDaters™ Seeking?

Previous chapters have presented information about three important questions:

1. How do you feel about dating?
2. What qualities are you looking for in a person to date?
3. Where would you most likely find someone to date?

    This chapter is going to look into the type of relationship you and other LaterDaters™ would like to have with someone. There are more relationship options available to us today than there were when we were in our twenties, as seen in this next letter.

Independent writes:

I like my independence, but I like a steady sweetheart too. My care-taking days are over because I am single and my kids have families of their own. At sixty-eight years of age, I don't even want a cat anymore, but I do want a man. My problem is that men my age seem to have agendas that don't square with mine. Where is the guy who is willing to live in his own house and do his own laundry? I just want to see him on Saturday night for a movie, maybe some dinner (out), and a sleepover. If he would take a few trips with me every year, that would be a real bonus. Marriage is not in my future. Just the thought of writing up an eighty-two page pre-nuptial to protect my assets scares me to death (little joke there). Men seem to be needy and insecure. Are they afraid I'm going to have two other guys on the side? Please. I don't have the energy for multiples.

Dear Independent:

You seem to want to keep your life as simple as possible, but adding a sweetheart will not accomplish that goal. The good news is that it will make your life fuller. The even better news is that the majority of men over the age of fifty are looking for just the kind of relationship you are seeking—steady and exclusive dating. Read chapter eight and take a deep breath. Start by checking steady/exclusive dating below.

Best wishes, Linda

What Kind of Relationships are You Looking For?

Please get out your pencil again and answer the following survey question. Lots of other single people over fifty did it and found it helpful.

Which of the following would be ideal relationships for you? (check all that apply)

- ☐ Marriage
- ☐ Steady/Exclusive Dating
- ☐ Dating Several People
- ☐ Friend for Travel and Events
- ☐ Having a Lover
- ☐ Single and Loving It

Men and women date for a wide variety of reasons, but at our age, almost no one is planning to start a family. We're out there looking for companionship, friendship, romance, love, sex, and maybe even marriage. We have every right to do this, but because it's such a historically new trend, most of us don't know how to do it very well.

Trish McDermot, president of romance for Match.com, stated, "more than one in five believe they'll find romance in a year." That sounds like romantic optimism to me—not practical facts. Statistics show that we are successful when we hunt, but lots of us LaterDaters™ are resigned to watching Letterman alone because we don't want to make the effort and possibly fail. An alarming 36 percent of single people in their fifties admitted they hadn't been kissed or hugged even once in the last six months. This sad statistic works if you have chosen single and loving it, but the rest of us choose human closeness.

Are you able to clarify your relationship goals? If you can figure out what you want from this adult dating circus, you'll save lots of precious time. By the third date with someone, you should have determined if he or she is an acceptable partner in terms of your goals. Now you need to find out what his or her goals might be. Are both of you seeking the same type of relationship? Bingo! If you have opposing relationship goals, don't waste each other's time. Using someone just to fill some empty time in your life is unfair to them, and your time could be better spent looking for the right person. I think men are more decisive than women in choosing to continue a relationship or move on to someone else. This could be due to the census numbers—men have more women to choose from and women have fewer men to date.

Let's think back to high school. Remember that thirty-five, forty-five, fifty-five years ago, or more, most of us imagined ourselves happily married till death do us part. Somewhere along the way, our dream didn't come true. Some of us never married, some of us divorced, and some of us experienced the death of our spouse at an early age. While we've been experiencing this thing called life, many of us have developed new relationship dreams. Some survey respondents pointed out that I hadn't included living together in the list. I apologize for that error and hope you choose steady/exclusive dating as an appropriate substitution. I've heard that an estimated 1.2 million unrelated LaterDaters™ live together without getting married.

What Kind of Relationships are Other Later Daters™ Looking For?

Sixty-nine percent of the two hundred survey respondents indicated that their goals included a steady and exclusive dating relationship. This was the same for both men and women.

TABLE 8.1: RELATIONSHIP GOALS RELATED TO GENDER

Relationship Goals ▽	100 Women	100 Men
Marriage	45%	47%
Steady Exclusive Dating	**69%**	**69%**
Dating Several People	9%	12%
Friend for Travel and Events	**57%**	46%
Having a Lover	24%	**58%**
Single and Loving It	26%	14%

Respondents could choose multiple categories.
• Bold numbers indicate goals selected by more that half of the respondents.

Respondents also chose marriage as a relationship goal in similar numbers (45 percent and 47 percent). Dating several people was reported as a goal by only 9 percent of the women and 12 percent of the men. Having a friend for travel and events was high for women (57 percent) and almost as high for men (46 percent). There is a very large divide existing between the number of women wanting a lover (24 percent) and the number of men with the same desire (58 percent). Women are single and loving it at almost twice the rate of men—26 percent compared to 14 percent.

The conclusions that can be drawn from this are that both men and women in this sample favor exclusive relationships. About 20 percent of the respondents selected exclusive dating over marriage. About half of the men and women chose a friend for travel and events as a goal.

Dating several people at the same time wasn't selected as a relationship goal by many.

Do relationship goals look different as we move from the fifty-year age range to the seventy-five-plus age range? The next chart should help answer this question.

TABLE 8.2 RELATIONSHIP GOALS RELATED TO AGE

Age ▶ Relationship Goals ▼	50-55 N=45	56-60 N=57	61-65 N=47	66-70 N=30	71-75 N=13	75 + N=8
Marriage	**58%**	**51%**	40%	40%	31%	25%
Steady/Exclusive Dating	**69%**	**70%**	**70%**	**60%**	**77%**	**75%**
Dating Several People	7%	7%	17%	13%	8%	13%
Friend for Travel and Events	31%	**54%**	**57%**	**70%**	**54%**	38%
Having a Lover	31%	35%	**53%**	43%	**54%**	38%
Single and Loving It	16%	12%	26%	27%	23%	38%

N = number of respondents.
Respondents could choose multiple categories.
Bold numbers indicate goals selected by more than half of the respondents.

With forty-five people in the 50–55 age category, we have two clear preferred choices: steady/exclusive dating at 69 percent, and marriage at 58 percent. Dating several people was not a goal for most people (7 percent) in this age group. A friend for travel/events matches having a lover at 31 percent. Sixteen percent reported to be single and loving it.

The 56–60 age group also indicates a preference for steady/exclusive relationships (70 percent), followed by marriage (51 percent).

Dating several people is still the least common goal. There is a significant rise in wanting a friend for travel and events (54 percent), while having a lover (35 percent) and loving being single (12 percent) are very close to the first age group.

The 61–65 age group shows a significant decline in having an interest in getting married (40 percent), but maintains its high interest in an exclusive relationship (70 percent). Dating several people is still low, but the highest approval rating of any of the age groups at 17 percent. Having a lover becomes much more acceptable at 53 percent of the forty-seven people in that age group choosing it. Having a friend for travel and events remained high at 57 percent. Being single is looking much better (26 percent) than it did to the two younger age groups.

The 66–70 age group surprisingly chooses a friend for travel and events (70 percent) over steady exclusive dating (60 percent), while marriage slipped to the 40 percent level. Dating several people is still the loser at 13 percent. Of the thirty people in that age level, 43 percent choose having a lover and 27 percent were sticking to their guns at being single and loving it.

There were only thirteen survey takers in the 71–75 age group, and they gave marriage a very low (31 percent) choice and gave steady exclusive dating a very high 77 percent. An equal percentage (54 percent) chose both having a friend for travel and events and having a lover. In this age group, 23 percent are single and loving it.

The over seventy-five age group was represented by only eight people. Many were asked, but few wanted to answer my survey. The eight people reported a strong desire (75 percent) for a steady exclusive dating relationship, and a weak desire for marriage (25 percent). The figure that appeared in three categories was 38 percent—friend for travel and events, having a lover, and single and loving it. The big loser in relationship choices reflected all the other age groups—only 13 percent chose dating several people.

The changes in the preferred relationships over time are easy to see. The desire to marry declines with age, while the desire to have a steady exclusive dating relationship remains high. Dating several people seems to be the least favored of relationships in all age groups. Having a friend for travel and events increases until the age group of 71–75, when it starts a downhill slide. Having a lover is a low choice among the youngest and oldest age categories. Single and loving it seems to grow in popularity as people age. You could conclude from this that if marriage is your goal, don't wait. As you and your potential dating partners age, this choice becomes less desirable to both of you.

How did your relationship history relate to the identified goals of our survey takers? The answer to this question can be found in table 8.3. If you've never been married, can we assume that you never want to marry? If you've been married three times, will you be more or less likely to try it again?

TABLE 8.3 RELATIONSHIP GOALS RELATED TO THE NUMBER OF TIMES MARRIED

Times Married ▶ Relationship Goals ▼	0 Times N=30	1 Time N=123	2 Times N=43	3 Times N=4
Marriage	37%	46%	**51%**	50%
Steady Exclusive Dating	**57%**	**73%**	**63%**	**100%**
Dating Several People	13%	7%	19%	0%
Friend for Travel and Events	43%	**55%**	47%	50%
Having a Lover	43%	43%	35%	25%
Single and Loving It	20%	19%	26%	0%

N = number of respondents.
Respondents could choose multiple categories.
Bold numbers indicate goals selected by more than half of the respondents.

It appears that the more times survey respondents had been married, the more they indicated a marriage or a steady exclusive dating relationship as a goal. It is possible that if marriage or an exclusive dating relationship was desirable in your past, it continues to be your relationship of choice for the future.

Dating several people was identified as a relationship goal by the smallest number of people in each of the six age groups. It is possible that dating several people is viewed by some LaterDaters™ as a means to an end—the goal being steady/exclusive dating or marriage.

Having a friend for travel and events was identified as a goal by 43 to 55 percent across all four groups. Having a lover was selected by 43 percent of the people who had never been married or had been married once. This choice was selected by fewer of the survey participants who had been married two or three times (35 and 25 percent).

Nineteen and 20 percent of those people who had never been married, or had been married once, indicated that they are single and loving it. Twenty-six percent who had been married twice selected single and loving it. None of the people who have been married three times (only four in the survey) identified single and loving it as a goal.

The numbers in all three charts about relationship seem to tell a story of a large group of LaterDaters™ who want a sweetheart or spouse in their lives and a small group who are single and loving it. Keep in mind, survey participants were found while actively participating in the dating world. Many of these energetic LaterDaters™ also included their own stories with their survey answers. Some of these stories follow.

Your Stories

Marriage

A woman in the 50–55 age category told this story of different dating goals. "I dated a seemingly, no truly, wonderful gentleman, who over time had indicated I had everything he's ever wanted in a woman. Because he was a sweetheart inside, I fell for him hook, line, and sinker. To me, he was the first soul mate I'd ever known, and my heart found its home. After acknowledging my words of affirmation to him about his positive attributes, he ran away. I was in shock and finally realized there is truly a fear of commitment. It was still worth the experience."

Another woman in the 50–55 age group has the goal of marriage. "I recently ended a 4-½ year relationship. We were the same age, best friends, and lovers. We were engaged. He was my buddy. With the passing of time, I realized I could not marry this person. Then I realized I would not even be able to live with him. I thought I could be happy and feel satisfied dating him exclusively the rest of my life. Soon I realized I didn't want that either. What I learned about myself is that my highest goal is marriage, and I need to be in a relationship with someone where I have that *hope*. Although I am alone now, I am in a place of *hope* to find a man who will be my husband. I never had an orgasm with my husband of sixteen years. It was after I was divorced that I finally experienced that wonderful excitement!"

Steady/Exclusive Dating

This appeared to be the winning relationship choice, but alas, no one wrote a story about it. Perhaps, singles in this type of relationship don't consider themselves to be single and therefore didn't take the survey and/or didn't add their stories.

Dating Several People

When my adult daughters say they are dating someone, what they really mean is that they are being intimate, and it is an exclusive relationship. When I say I am dating someone, it means nothing of the sort. This dating word seems to have many different definitions. The majority of my adult dating (I'll add up the numbers someday) did not involve sex, and it did not imply that I wasn't going out with others. Those relationships that I have had that became serious and involved sex became monogamous, or I got out of them. You probably think going out with three or four people in the same week is crazy. I consider it a market survey. You may think that having sex with three or four people in one week is great. I consider it sleazy and dangerous to one's health. It all depends on what you want at the end of your dating experiences. I want to marry Mr. Wonderful, and I don't think he would want Mrs. Wonderful to have had sex with everyone she has dated. The survey results certainly show me to be the odd duck. Very few people indicated that they wanted to date several people at the same time. Maybe they associate the word date with the word sex too.

A gentleman in the 66–70 age group writes about dating several people at the same time. "We all need to learn how to sort our opportunities—age, beauty, religion, politics, etc. Finding your mate will probably require multiple dating, as dating one at a time may take forever with little or no results, many false starts, not to mention cost. I believe that many of the profiles shown on the various sites are inaccurate and waste your time. People who are active on-line should always respond either positively or negatively to let the other know that they are still active on-line. Short periods of time at any one site (one month) will provide all the opportunities available on that site. If you contact several persons at a time, you will save money. After a month, move to a new site or come back to past sites after three or four months."

Friend for Travel and Events

A man in the 66–70 age group wrote about developing friendships through dating. "To me, dating is a pain. I've had many female friends these past twenty-six years and lots of activity. A few got serious, and I think I missed the boat a couple times. Now looking for a rich widow and considering checking some old flames." He added this funny story. "I won a brief membership in 'Together' (I think they needed guys). There were ten gals who sent me their data, photos, etc. I met five. The first one, she was looking for Mr. Right, and after talking on the phone, said I didn't sound as if I wanted to get serious. 'But,' I said, 'we ought to at least meet for pie as we had talked for an hour.' We found we had a lot in common and started dating. I went through her crises with other men. We've been best friends for nineteen years and mutually helpful in many ways. She's been through cancer, two knee replacements, and piles of stuff. She's retired and we see each other less, but each is there for the other, for fun or whatever. That's better than dating."

Having a Lover

This choice was more popular with men than with women. However, no one was willing to share a story about their lover. Discretion is a valuable quality, and I'm gratified that the survey respondents used it.

Single and Loving It

A woman in the 71–75 age group would like a friend for travel and events, but is okay with being single. "Because my history is a bit irregular (ages 18–42 in the convent), my dates sort themselves into 'way too interested in my *old* life' to 'thought I was born on the day I met them'. One gentleman, a rock-ribbed Protestant, might as well have taken notes. He wanted *details*. At the other extreme was a self-centered, successful gent who never showed even the remotest interest in my past. In the course of a three-year relationship, we visited (in an almost shrine-like reverence) everywhere he had ever lived. And so it ended, with my actually asking him if he thought I was born on the day I met him. My never having been married makes me not such a great catch either, and the fact that I'd really like a male friend who would be collapsible and easily shelved—content to be taken out when I so wished—may tell the final tale—so it continues…single and okay with it!"

A woman in the 50–55 age group has two ideal relationships in mind—married or single and loving it. "My first dating relationship was eight months after separating. He was the polar opposite of my ex-spouse—controlling and flirty. It went for four months, and I did not get sexually involved, and I ended it. After a couple more short-term stints, I met a man who was also separated. He was cute and handy but had problems that included snoring, sleep apnea, and ED, and so our eighteen-month relationship ended. Since then, my life included a year-long relationship with a person I didn't love, and a three-year sabbatical from romance that was followed by a two-month relationship. These looked serious, but problems arose. Now I am happily single again and not looking. There is too much baggage at our age. I don't like ex-spouses, kids, grandkids (I have none), etc. My life is peaceful, pleasant, and I don't feel like I need, or maybe even want, another guy around all of the time. I don't want to take care of them, change them, or deal with their issues!" Signed, "Happy to be Free."

A gentleman in the 50–55 age group writes that he wants to stay single. "Being voted most shy in my high school graduating class is a label no one wants. Since then, I've become a dancer (Ballroom, Latin, Swing). I have no problems getting a date now. My problem today is asking a dance partner for a non-dance date without getting into a relationship. I let them know: this is just light dating—we are going out for a fun time, we are not in an exclusive relationship, planning a wedding date, or having sex. I feel that having no kids may make a difference. I was engaged eleven years ago, but a month before our wedding day she passed away."

A safe conclusion to draw from this chapter about the types of relationships that LaterDaters™ want is wide ranging depending on their sex, age, and times married. Try and determine by the third meeting what that other person wants in a relationship. Don't ever think that you can change their mind about their relationship goals.

Look back to page 74 and write the types of relationships you are seeking here. _____
_____
_____
_____
_____
_____

The three charts in this chapter tell us loudly and strongly that the most sought after relationship, regardless of gender, age category, or times married is steady/exclusive dating. By choosing this type of relationship, I think people feel they can enjoy all the positives they know are available to them—having a lover and having a friend for travel and events. This relationship avoids some of the negatives people may have experienced in the past: the possible need to go through a divorce, the worry that your sweetheart is dating others, and the sharing of finances and living space that is necessary in a marriage. If you have chosen steady exclusive dating as one of your relationship options, you will be able to find many LaterDaters™ that share that same goal.

If marriage is your goal (45 percent of women and 47 percent of men in my sample), you should try and get to that Little Chapel in Vegas as soon as possible, because the desire for that type of relationship may decrease with age. About half of the people who have been married one, two, or three times say they would be willing to do that again. Convincing someone who is over fifty and never married to change their stripes and marry you may be hard to do as only 37 percent of those in my survey indicated that they wanted to get married.

Dating several people was the least common relationship goal. You may desire this situation, but you're going to have a hard time finding people who have the same goal.

If you are seeking a friend for travel and events, you are in luck because of the LaterDaters™ surveyed 57 percent of women and 46 percent of men are looking for you too. The retired people (ages 66–70) are eager (70 percent) to spend some fun time with you.

Having a lover was selected as a relationship goal by 58 percent of men surveyed, but they are going to have to do some fast-talking because only 24 percent of the women choose this.

Many of you have read about those "Happiness Tests" that state the following:

Happiest people = married men
Next happiest   = single women
Next happiest   = married women
Least happy   = unmarried men

Our survey didn't ask this question specifically, but the findings appear consistent with the happiness test since 26 percent of the women chose single and loving it while only 14 percent of the men did so.

I think you are reading this book because you, like the majority of single people over fifty, want a relationship other than the one you are currently experiencing—being single. The only way to change your relationship status is to do some dating. You may have to make some changes in your life to accommodate this new dating you, and change requires action on your part. The remaining chapters in this book will help you get into action.

Reflections on Chapter Eight

- The relationship goal that most surveyed LaterDaters™ chose (at 69 percent) was steady exclusive dating. It remained the top choice in all age categories and by all the time-married groups.
- Fifty-eight percent of the men chose having a lover, while only 24 percent of the women did.
- Forty-five percent of the women and 47 percent of the men surveyed identified marriage as a goal. Fewer people identified marriage as a goal in the older age groups.

- Having a friend for travel and events was chosen by 57 percent of the women and 46 percent of the men.
- Remember that marriage or steady exclusive dating usually comes with the built-in benefits of having a lover and a friend for travel and events.

PART THREE

LaterDating™ Tips

"A man can sleep around, no questions asked, but if a woman makes nineteen or twenty mistakes, she's a tramp."
Joan Rivers

CHAPTER NINE

♥

> Does my hair make me look fat?

> She was probably expecting a Lexus not my old Pacer.

> No one can make you feel inferior without your consent.

Would You Date You?

Appearance Counts for Both Men and Women

I would like to believe that I have grown up and no longer judge people by appearance, but it happens. Someone who is physically attractive has social and professional advantages. Those advantages are erased if that person has an unpleasant personality. But, most men and women make snap judgements on someone's first appearance, so let's start there. When you walk into a party, meeting, or a job interview, do you feel confident that your appearance is polished and appropriate?

What does a male need to do to be polished and well groomed? Good hygiene requires more than a three-minute shower in the morning. Go the extra mile and get a good haircut. I don't know any woman who likes a comb over, a bad toupee, or a hairline that blends into the hair that grows on your back. There is absolutely nothing wrong with bald, especially if the hair around the bald area is kept short. A good barber should trim any hair you may have growing from your ears or your nostrils. Ask them to take care of that problem, or you will risk looking much older than your years. Many men think they look good with some facial hair. A well-defined mustache or beard can be attractive, but a scraggly one isn't. Clean and trimmed fingernails, clean teeth and breath, and polished shoes always serve you well. Fashions for men don't seem to change rapidly, but if you're wearing something that is more than ten years old, it may be time to upgrade. The only exception to this might be a tuxedo or a really great coat.

Good hygiene should be at the top of every woman's list too. Women also have to consider things like make-up. We need it, but it shouldn't look like a mask. There are many department and cosmetic stores that offer good advice and free make-up demonstrations. Take advantage of these services. Hair makes a big difference in any woman's appearance too. Many men like long hair, but most women over fifty don't look good in long hair. A good hairdresser can solve this contradiction. Your nails need to be clean and filed—polished or not. Choose clothing that is appropriate for both your age and your lifestyle. It may be difficult, but it's important to choose clothing that isn't too tight and sexy while avoiding clothing that's too baggy and dowdy looking. Solving these clothing dilemmas requires careful thought and planning until you understand what compliments your figure and lifestyle. If you know someone who always seems to look stylish, I'm sure she would be complimented if you asked her where she buys her lovely outfits.

Judging a man or a woman by appearance may seem to be a superficial and shallow test, but, unfortunately, most of us judge and are judged initially by our exteriors.

If you polish up your exterior, more people will want to learn about your interior—your positive attitude, interests, and energy. Moreover, if you are confident that your appearance is pleasing, you will be more at ease in social and business situations. A confidant and interesting person is someone who attracts others to them and is someone who is able to approach others with a smile. You can be that person because you're no longer an insecure teenager. You've developed social skills through years of practice. Your sense of self is so much greater now than it was when you were in your twenties. The interesting adult that you've become should not hide behind a crumpled or bland exterior. Your exterior appearance and behavior should be as shiny and polished as your interior.

Rate That Date: Judge Yourself as a Date

Think of the last date you either enjoyed or endured. Now get out your pen or pencil and judge yourself on that date.

Did you look your best? See the past section, and be honest. _____
_____
_____

Did you show up with a smile, leave with a smile, and laugh in between?
_____
_____

Did you give a compliment to the other person? _____
_____
_____

Did you keep the conversation flowing, or did it drag? _____
_____
_____

Did most of your sentences start with the word "I"? _____
_____
_____

Did you seem enthusiastically interested in the other person's life?____
_____

Did you do any over-sharing of information about past romances or marriages? _____
_____

Did you complain about this, that, or the other thing? _____
_____
_____

Did you thank the person for the date? _____
_____

Now ask yourself the question again. Would you date you? _____
_____

What do you convey on a date? _____
_____
_____
_____
_____
_____

Traits

Perhaps you had difficulty filling out that part of the Rate That Date list that asked you to state what you conveyed on your last date. If so, I would like you to look at the following list from the viewpoint of someone you have dated. Circle some positive traits and some negative traits that someone would choose to describe you.

POSITIVES	NEGATIVES
Happy	Depressed
Attractive	Slovenly
Interested and curious	Uninterested and self-centered
Non-judgmental	Prejudiced
Good sense of humor	Boorish
Self-confident	Arrogant
Kindhearted	Mean spirited
Well-spoken	Foul-mouthed

    You just circled some reasons your last sweetie really enjoyed you and some reasons why he or she didn't. Perhaps you know a little more about yourself now. Are you able to re-make yourself into the most perfect, wonderful, and amazing date anyone has ever had? Probably not. However, we are all able to make some changes in our behavior—or at least try. We've all made changes in our lives during the last fifty, sixty, or seventy years. Every one of us has encountered problems and overcome them through our lifetime, again and again.

Those negative traits that you circled above should not be considered a roadblock to your dating success. Remember, you've had lots of practice making changes. To remind yourself of your own strength, make a list of some of the problems you've overcome in your life.

_____
_____
_____
_____
_____
_____
_____

Give Yourself Credit

If it was easy to find negative words to describe your dating self and difficult to find positive words about yourself, stop right now and give yourself some credit. Many women are so used to devaluing themselves that they usually overlook their good qualities and focus on their faults. Me, too. Women are concerned about how they do, or do not, measure up to others. Women have very little understanding of the fears older men have—the fear of rejection and erectile dysfunction (Gross 2000). If you have confidence that you are an attractive person—physically, emotionally, and intellectually—you will be able to enrich someone else's life. You are over fifty and you know what life is about now. When you were twenty, did you have any idea about life, self-esteem, or the value of love and companionship? Today, after many of life's hard lessons, you are wiser, and, hopefully, more forgiving about your own and others' shortcomings.

Basic Instincts

This chapter would be incomplete without looking again at what qualities men and women are seeking in a date (chapter six). In that chapter we learned that for our surveyed LaterDaters™ the most sought after quality for both sexes was similar interests. Women listed this quality 88 percent of the time and men listed it 85 percent of the time. After that brief moment of similarity, we reach the great divide. Some stereotypes seem to be based on reality. The men choose physically attractive 83 percent of the time and women choose intelligent (87 percent), kindhearted (86 percent), and financially secure (81 percent) of the time. Financially secure doesn't necessarily mean wealthy; it could mean secure and comfortable. So let's say it as it is: men like attractive women, and women like intelligent, kind, financially secure men. I don't think this means men are shallow and only consider the appearance of a woman. It also doesn't mean that women are gold diggers, only looking for some smart, rich man who is willing to be kind to them. I actually have a more reasonable explanation for these numbers. You may not agree with my cave people reasoning, but here goes.

We have lived in houses for about ten thousand years, and before that, we lived in caves for about two hundred thousand years. Pretend you are a caveman looking for a mate. You would logically choose a woman who appears healthy and strong. Studies have shown that men still operate with that caveman philosophy, whether they realize it or not. In contemporary society, healthy and strong translates to relatively slim, good posture, clear complexion, nice teeth, and well groomed.

Now, pretend you are a cave woman who is deciding between Fred and Barney. Fred has trouble catching a fish. Barney has proven he's a good hunter and regularly drags mastodon meat through the cave door. He is intelligent, and a good provider who is kindhearted. He would be able and willing to feed you and the baby. It's an easy choice. We humans are programmed to survive and reproduce. We can't erase these basic human instincts, even if single women over fifty in the twenty-first century can usually support themselves and single men over fifty usually don't want to start a family. Human instincts don't disappear because we have moved from caves to condos.

Now, another short test. Using the cave people theory, would you date you? Ladies, do you appear healthy—not overweight and not stick thin. Do you carry yourself with confidence or do you slump? Are you well groomed? Do you get your hair done by someone who understands color and style? Does your make-up enhance your good features. Are your clothes in style for someone your age?

Men have stated loudly and clearly that physically attractive is very important to them. What is that one physical feature that you hate about yourself? How many years have you despised your nose or your acne scars or your flat breasts or crooked teeth? Is it impossible for you to have that one physical feature that you despise changed? I'm not suggesting one of those TV total make-over slash and burn jobs. If there is one physical thing that bothers you daily, it is no doubt affecting your self-confidence and your ability to date. Then work up your courage, open your purse, and change it. You might find this decision very empowering. It could even change your life. Please refer back to page 52 for warnings about choosing a plastic surgeon.

Women have stated loudly and clearly that they want to date someone who is Mr. Intelligent/Kindhearted/Financially Secure man. This means different things to different people. It is unlikely that the women who filled out the survey were picturing a cross between Albert Einstein, Billy Graham, and Bill Gates. Maybe they are looking for someone who uses conventional grammar and doesn't kick the cat. Some women might feel a man is financially secure if he has a job and limited debt, while other women are looking for a brilliant money manager who has amassed a large stock portfolio and a pension plan. As a caveman, you have no way of knowing what a woman's expectations of you might be—does she need a guy who works hard at hunting and is willing to share or one who is smart enough to invent traps and has mastodon meat stored away?

Men who have lots of monetary assets are sometimes too willing to tell a woman all about them. This can be a turn-off to a self-sufficient woman who doesn't want to feel like she's being purchased. Finances are like sex in a relationship—you need to get there slowly. After you know one another fairly well, then fill in the details. But remember this: Cheap guys often lose the girl. Pick her up in a clean car and pay the dinner check. If you are short of cash, choose an inexpensive restaurant, and pay the entire tab. Go for a walk if you can't afford to pay for two dinners. If you ask a woman out for a movie, it's assumed you are going to buy the tickets and the popcorn. If a woman has asked you to a movie or out to dinner, a gentleman will at least offer to pay his half of the bill. Don't start thinking about the money your former wife cost you. This woman you are dating needs to be impressed with your financial security, and your kindhearted intelligence. Her cave woman brain needs to know that she will be fed and kept warm in the winter because her caveman is capable and generous.

Sex Too Soon

Now, I want to have a candid talk with you, a single woman over fifty. If you're a man reading this book, you can just skip this paragraph. None of us are virgins and all of us know that men like sex. Having said that, I believe women make a big mistake by having sex too early in a relationship. I have heard stories from men that make me ashamed of my gender. One man told me about being invited to a woman's apartment after their first date only to have the woman appear naked from her kitchen carrying drinks! She followed that act by having sex with him on the floor. Most men will not turn down sex, but more than this one man has told me they don't continue to date any woman who has sex with them on the first three dates. Why? Because they figure you are a woman who has sex too quickly with everyone you date. They think you are promiscuous and fear that you might have a few STDs to boot. Please don't skip the important parts of courtship. Courtship should include sharing humor, experiences, histories, interests, and opinions. Don't undervalue yourself. Any women can offer sex, but you have so much more to offer. Save sex for the frosting on the cake.

If you're a man who wants to impress a woman, be patient with your sexual desires. If you are able to make a woman feel valued and respected for her non-sexual qualities, she will think you are the *Time* magazine man of the year. Becoming friends before you become lovers will make the intimacy that much more relaxed and wonderful. Any anxiety issues you may have developed over the years will be much easier to talk about with a friend than with someone who's name you don't quite remember. If the only thing you want from your relationship with a woman is sex, choose a professional, and spare the heart of an unsuspecting lady. She deserves more.

CHAPTER TEN

♥

Flirting

What Does Flirting Look Like?

Flirt 1. To court thrillingly or act amorously without serious intentions; play at love; coquet (*Random House College Dictionary*, 1982).

When the famous anthropologist Margaret Mead studied flirting in various cultures around the world, she saw clear courtship patterns. If you approached adulthood in one of the traditional societies Mead studied, you spent years observing how to do it and how to interpret every nuance of courtship behavior. She also noted that in the United States there wasn't a mutual understanding of flirting or courtship cues (Mead 1949).

More recent studies have discovered some universal flirting patterns that would surprise Margaret, and might surprise you. Using a camera that had a bogus lens pointing forward and a working, but hidden, lens on the side, a German named Irenaus Eibl-Eibesfeldt traveled the world in the 1960s observing flirting behaviors in many cultures. He observed female flirting in places as far removed from one another as the jungles of the Amazon to the cafes of Paris. He described a pattern of flirting that was so similar, he concluded it was innate.

What do women do when they flirt? The woman smiles and lifts her eyebrows in a swift motion as she opens her eyes wide to look at him. Then she drops her eyelids, tilts her head down to the side, and looks away. She will often cover her face with her hands and giggle. This seemingly silly and coquettish behavior seems to be the world norm for women (Fischer 1992).

What do men do when they flirt? They thrust out their chests. This simple move can be observed on any street corner, beach, or bar, and also seems to be universal. When a man wants to make himself noticed by a certain woman, he will suck in his belly and push out his chest (Fischer 1992).

Signaling mutual interest between the sexes is referred to as the copulatory gaze. This two-to-three-second stare is observed in Western cultures but not in cultures where eye contact between the sexes is not permitted. During this mating stare, pupils may dilate. This stare then requires some sort of action on the part of the participants—they can either retreat or approach one another. After the initial staring, if either or both of the participants are showing a toothy smile, they are indicating an even stronger interest in each other. This means that when you notice someone staring, you need to instantly decide if you want to give him or her a big smile. If you wait or pretend you're too busy, you miss out on meeting someone who has shown that they find you attractive.

If you and I had known about these flirting rituals during high school, we could have saved ourselves a lot of pain and embarrassment. We could've read one another's cues and realized that the person we had the big crush on probably wasn't—or was—interested in us. Well, that time has passed, and now we need to decide how we are going to flirt as single adults in our fifties, sixties, seventies, and beyond.

We've learned that there seems to be universal flirting rituals. You may wonder if these attraction cues change with age. The simple answer is they probably don't change, but we may be more cautious in displaying them or in responding to them. By the time we're fifty, or into our sixties and seventies, we have probably experienced many romantic relationships. We no longer fit into that U.S. average of young people marrying their third serious dating partner. You could say we've had more time to do market research, and tried multiple flirting methods. We approach flirting with a longer history of triumphs and disappointments in the dating world. There is always that risk of being humiliated when our flirtations are rebuffed, but keep your chin up. You can always notice someone across the room with whom you *must* talk.

When Our Flirting Falls Flat

I am reminded of those junior high school dances, with the boys lined up on one wall and the girls lined up on the opposite wall. A young man gets up his nerve to walk the long walk across the gym floor and ask a girl to dance. If she says no, which is very likely because she only wants to dance with one specific boy in the entire school, the brave young man has to do the walk of shame back to the boys' side of the gym. Everyone has seen his failure, and he doesn't forget the rejection for the rest of his life. At the same time, there are girls standing on their side of the gym who are enduring the shame of never being asked to dance, and they never forget that feeling of rejection either.

Sometimes we think someone is flirting with us, only to find out differently. My favorite guffaw took place when a woman friend and I were sitting on bar stools that turned away from the bar and toward the band we came to hear. There was a very attractive man sitting at a table by the band who repeatedly looked my way. I smiled at him, but he didn't ask me to dance, or come over to talk to me. He continued to look, and I continued to smile without results. Finally, in desperation—when he was looking my direction—I waved at him, no response. It took me another ten minutes to realize that he wasn't looking at little egotistical me, he was watching sports on the TV that was right over my head! If he really had been flirting with me, he would have smiled back at me. I learned there needs to be a reciprocal exchange of flirting cues, and that it's easy to misinterpret those cues if I you're overly anxious to flirt with someone.

Flirting Skills Need a Pick-Me-Up

Adults have more social graces than do junior high students, but they don't relish rejection any more than a thirteen-year-old. Adult single dances can be a very comfortable place to flirt. A man can ask someone to dance easily enough, and the women have come to the dance looking forward to saying yes to a dance request. Women who arrive with a cohort of lady friends and sit around a table in the corner farthest from the action will probably dance far less than the woman who walks through the crowd ("oops, excuse me, haven't I seen you at one of these dances before?"). Single men and women who go to events designed for singles should take a risk, get up out of their chairs, put a smile on their faces, and realize they're at a party, not a gripe session.

My best flirting invention is called the "five-second smile." If I make eye contact with a man that I find attractive, I will give him a big smile (lots of teeth) for a complete five seconds. I count in my head, one potato, two potato, etc. At the end of the five seconds, this guy knows I am flirting with him. He knows that I find him attractive. He has two possible responses: positive or negative. If it's positive, he will smile back at me and then walk over and begin a conversation because he knows his chances of being rejected are very low. If his reaction is negative, he will look away. This is not the end of my world. All I have lost is five seconds of my life. My pride is still intact because I have not made that walk across the gym floor; I have not tried to come up with some cutesy pick-up line, and he and I are the only people who know he just rejected my flirting.

Usually guys are expected to initiate flirting. Men tell me that they are used to being rejected. It can be hurtful, but they have trained for it since the kindergarten kick-ball team lottery, little league, college applications, job interviews, and innumerable unsuccessful attempts at flirting with women they consider attractive. You've got to hand it to guys—they usually think flirting is worth a try. Most women tend to be passive about flirting. They might know how to respond, but they usually don't feel comfortable initiating it. Take a risk!

Flirting should never be rushed. If either party appears to be too aggressive, it will probably end the courting process. Don't get too close or touch too soon or talk too much because it is very likely that the other person will be repelled by what appears to be pushy or manic behavior (Fischer 1992). The five-second smile avoids these pitfalls because it doesn't involve closeness, touching, or talking.

You have probably already guessed that I'm an extrovert. You may believe that you are an introvert and that the five-second smile would be something you could never use. There have been many times when I was very attracted to someone and was too shy to pull the smile trick. I regret those missed chances. More important, I have learned that there are some places where I feel comfortable flirting—anyplace with good old rock 'n roll music.

You need to find a venue that is comfortable for you and where other single people your age also feel comfortable. Many adults feel at ease using an Internet dating service for making initial contacts that might lead to a coffee date or another informal meeting. This method allows you to do some virtual flirting and avoids the risk of face-to-face rejection, at least until you actually meet. Being introduced to someone by a friend or relative is also comfortable for most people because it's usually preceded by agreement of both of the daters. Attending singles interest groups, like tennis or bridge or maybe a book club, can be less intimidating than a singles dance because it doesn't require you to find a partner in order to participate.

Don't Quit Flirting

Rejection hurts, but by the time you are as old as I am, you, like me, have probably been rejected in one way or another many times. We lived through it. What have we learned from all of these hurtful experiences? Some of the two hundred people I surveyed learned that if they gave up their quest for a relationship, they could avoid the hurt of rejection. (If you don't play the game, you can't lose the game.) However, the majority of the people surveyed have continued to seek a special relationship even though it requires flirting, and therefore, the risk of rejection. We should assure ourselves that flirting is a universal behavior that sometimes has wonderful results.

Flirting advice can be summed up in two words: be friendly. How do you react to a smiling person who gives you a cheery "hi"? Most of us primates mimic that action with a returned smile and a returned "hi." We usually don't jump to the conclusion that we are dealing with a serial killer. What normal person doesn't respond positively to a friendly person? What's wrong with continuing this simple interaction with a "How are you today"? Almost anything you say while smiling will be well received. Smiles make other people happy and open to conversation.

Your happiness is contagious and is best spread in person—not through those little emoticons on email. By being friendly, you are communicating to someone that they are worthy of your interest.

Once a person has responded to your friendly behaviors, you can continue to the next level of flirting. This next level requires you to connect with that person's statements by validating them, and then to connect to their feelings by using sympathetic body language. This level of flirting is just another indication of being friendly. For example, what if someone says they are excited because they have just purchased a new hybrid car or become a grandparent or are planning a trip? Those potential conversation starters would be stopped by any of the following: those cars are overpriced, or grandkids get to be a nuisance, or I've been there and hated it. Friendlier responses might begin with words like: "That's so exciting because…, so wonderful because…, so much fun because…" All of these phrases indicate that you are a friendly person who finds their life interesting. No, it isn't fawning flattery. It is socially acceptable friendly flirting.

If you're still feeling a bit uncomfortable, I hope it is comforting to know that flirting is a universal practice, and that it's just friendliness. Yes, you can be rejected, but plan for success.

CHAPTER ELEVEN

Dating Dilemmas I Have Encountered and You May Too

Placing My Big Foot In My Big Mouth

This book has already mentioned ways that people never make it to the second date—posting inaccurate information and photos on-line comes to mind, as does being poorly groomed. But there is another easy way to botch a date. It's easy to talk yourself out of a chance for a second date on the very first date by choosing controversial topics to talk about. The first date can be a getting-to-know-you game. The game rules are tricky because you need to show interest in your date's life. If you don't, a date may think that you're not interested in him or her. However, beware of getting too personal too quickly. There are topics that many people consider to be their business, and they don't want to share them on a first date. Money, politics, and religion are three of these prickly topics. The problem comes if you show too much interest in things the other person doesn't want to share. This becomes a delicate balancing act because different people have different taboo topics.

The big issues people should try to avoid on a first date are any questions that might make the other person think you are trying to find out information about their financial status. Questions about employment, educational attainments, or where they live could raise some red flags in people's minds.

I've stringently followed this rule, but sometimes it backfires because guys think I'm not interested in their lives. Many people closely identify themselves with their work and they can't imagine having a conversation that doesn't include that subject. Every first date I've ever had has told me what he does for his job—I didn't have to ask. After your date tells you about their working life, it's easy to build a conversation from there. Ask such questions as, "How long have you been in that line of work," or "What do you enjoy doing when you're not at work?" People don't want to feel like they are going through a credit check on a first date, so avoid giving any indication that you're prying into their financial lives.

Attempt to avoid the two other bombs—religion and politics. What are the chances that two people are going to have the same philosophies on these topics? Don't put these cards on the table during a first date. I've saved this information for a third date and have still been eliminated from future dates. As a rabid Democrat who doesn't identify herself with any religion, you may understand my dilemma. My honesty has frightened off many suitors because their philosophies are at odds with mine. I've learned that being straightforward on the topics of religion and politics too early in a dating relationship often stops that relationship dead in its tracks.

We like to think that there aren't social classes in the United States, but when push comes to shove, we seem to choose friends from our same financial and educational level. Dating isn't any different. Most people are comfortable dating someone with a lifestyle similar to their own. When we were in high school or college, our financial futures were unclear. Now that we are in our fifties, sixties, and seventies, our educational and financial levels are usually obvious. This doesn't mean that the rich will find romance and the poor will find none. As an example, I am a financially comfortable woman with a good pension, no debt, and more investments than the average person. Wouldn't you think that men would find this attractive? However, a few men have told me that they don't want to date me anymore because "they could never afford what I have." The only men who seem comfortable with my finances are men who are in an even better financial position. This eliminates lots of great men from my dating pool. In this scenario, are cavemen trying to dominate cave women? I've also personally observed wealthy women choosing to date financially strapped men. Do these women want to be in control of the relationship? Maybe.

The lesson to be learned is what not to ask and what not to answer on the topics of money, religion, and politics. My younger daughter taught me something important when she said, " Be breezy, Mom." Sometimes it's really not what you say, but how you say it. If you sound like a district attorney when you ask questions, and like an evangelist or a politician when you answer questions, you will be breaking the breezy rule. Avoiding the heavy topics doesn't mean you can only talk about the weather, sports, movies, books, new restaurants, desired travel locations, funny life stories, and other non-controversial conversation topics. Just start your dating relationship with the light topics and save the heavy ones for later.

Am I Too Fussy? Or, Why Can't I Just Love This One?

If you've been dating for a number of years, you've probably had some serious romances and, possibly, some talk of marriage. Since you are reading this book, you must not have taken those romances into the future. That makes you as fussy as I am. I am a woman who says she wants to get married, but has turned down four marriage proposals. Do I think I'm so wonderful that only a prince qualifies to be my mate?

So why can't I just love the ones who love me? Those of you who are fifty are probably planning to live another forty years. Do you want to be alone all that time? I figure that I've got another thirty years to go, and I want to make them more fun by sharing them with a sweetie. Because most of us have already experienced marriage or long-term relationships, we know what we don't want, and we know what we do want, and we're afraid of making another mistake. We LaterDaters™ are often saddled with too much information about what we need to be happy in a relationship. This brand of perfectionism can keep us living alone.

Then there are those of us who, despite bad relationship experiences, remain hopelessly romantic. I remember reading an AARP article suggesting that older marriages tend to be more practical. The implication was that romance was not really what we LaterDaters™ were seeking, but rather someone with whom we could split the water bill. I agree that most of us are seeking a practical pairing, but most of us want more than that. We are also hoping for the magic that makes two people light up in each other's presence.

We've all lived long enough to know that love is not just a practical decision. However, that doesn't mean any of us should be blind to the deal breakers—addictions, financial irresponsibility, the personality of a stone, or children who seem possessed. To keep them fresh in your mind, jot down your own deal breakers here:

_____
_____
_____
_____
_____

Deal Breakers: Religion, Politics, and Smoking

Let's explore a scenario that has happened to many people: You're dating a wonderful person and a good relationship is beginning to develop. This sweetheart probably shares your interests and educational/financial levels. This might be the one! Our survey had indicated that a "Healthy Lifestyle" was very important to us LaterDaters™; similar religions and similar politics were not very important. However, the survey numbers don't tell the complete story when people have opposing views on religion and politics.

I was asked to attend a certain church with a man—and this invitation was on the first date. His intentions were noble, saving me from hell, but the resulting conversation wasn't pretty. Although I respect most religions (voodoo would not be included), conversion is not on my must-do list. If it becomes apparent early in a dating relationship that the two of you have opposing religious views, walk away. You're not going to change anyone's religious affiliation by discussion and compromise. In my opinion, it's impossible to apply logic to any belief system because they're all based on faith.

Politics, on the other hand (right or left), can be an interesting conversation stimulator between two reasonable people. Reasonable is defined here as someone who is actually willing to listen to another person's perspective before presenting evidence to the contrary. If you have extreme political beliefs and no tolerance for differing opinions, I would suggest sticking with your own clan. Do you really want to spend precious relationship time arguing? Walk away quickly.

Smoking can also be a deal breaker. Reformed smokers or non-smokers don't want to hang out in smoke-filled rooms. If you're a smoker and you're looking for someone to love, you might need to find another smoker. When we were in our twenties did anyone ever say, "I would never date that person, because they smoke"? But you hear it now. Our knowledge about the effects of smoking has increased, and our tolerance of it has proportionately decreased.

I told the man who was to become my second husband that I would not marry him unless he stopped smoking. He stopped, and we got married. Two months later I saw him in the back yard lighting up. When he died at the young age of fifty-four from a heart attack, he had smoked for forty years. Do you think I date smokers?

I'm sure you know of other deal breakers—gambling and flogging come to mind—but the big three seem to be religion, politics, and smoking. Why start a relationship with two strikes against you? If you have decided to overlook a big flaw in your sweetheart, you need to ask yourself why. Are you undervaluing yourself, are you lonely, or are you too lazy to keep looking? Don't settle for anything that you'll regret later.

Location, Location, Location

We all know how important location is in real estate, but have you thought about its effect on romance? I've heard many men say that they ended a relationship because the woman lived too far away, and they were sick of doing all the driving. Do you use an Internet dating service with the thought that you'll fall in love and move away from your home, children, grandchildren, and friends to live in another state? Probably not.

I moved from my condo in the city to my sweetheart's townhouse in a suburb. Our romance was going strong and even our housecleaning habits were compatible. Then the problem of location appeared. I didn't like the suburbs, and he didn't like the city. Neither one of us was willing to compromise. I moved back to my condo and that effectively ended the romance.

By the time we are LaterDaters™, we probably have achieved a certain comfort level with our surroundings—it can be difficult to move on. Single people in their fifties and sixties are probably less flexible about moving to a new location than they were in their twenties and thirties. We enjoy our neighborhoods. We don't want to move far away from our adult children and our workplace. However, this sometimes changes when people retire.

Most of the retired people I have ever dated brought up the topic of where they would like to live during the cold Minnesota winter. Many chose a warmer climate. More importantly, they want a partner for this new phase of their life. They were looking for someone who enjoyed the same activities they did: golf, tennis, fishing, travel, boating, and whatever else can be done in Minnesota in the summer, but requires a warm climate in the winter. Those retired people who live in Florida, Arizona, and any other warm state are probably looking for a cooler place to spend the months of May through September. Many of the retired LaterDaters™ are waiting to meet that special person to help them make the decision about where to spend that other half of the year. Changing locations to find what you consider to be good weather can be a desirable thing—but that home base can still be a point of contention.

Agreeing to Date a Mystery Person is a Mistake

This book contains many stories related to deceptions used in on-line dating, but this one takes the prize. A man who had an interesting profile, but no photo contacted me on Match.com. We emailed, talked on the phone, and agreed to meet for dinner. I received a phone call from him two hours before the planned dinner date. He changed the dinner date at a nice restaurant to a meeting at Culver's for dessert—yes, the burger and custard place. I had just been downgraded from dinner to custard. Not wanting to be rude, I met him at Culver's, only to discover that I already knew the guy. He had been very deceptive by doing a bait and switch with dinner and by remaining anonymous when he could have easily identified himself as someone I had previously met. I had been very accommodating by driving a long distance and agreeing to a drastic change in plans. The date lasted fifteen seconds. Then I said, "Why didn't you identify yourself as someone I had previously met? As far as I'm concerned, this date is over." Lesson learned: no photo means no date. You never know if that person you're emailing is your second cousin, or if the only photo of that person is on the post office wall.

Our Adult Children Put In Their Two Cents, Or More

By the time we have become LaterDaters™, most of us bring some baggage with us. The heaviest part of that baggage can be our children. These children are probably at least teenagers, and more likely, in their twenties, thirties, or forties. If our children are grown, we may have them looking over our shoulders. We spent many years giving them dating and mating advice. Now, it's their turn.

They want us to be happy, but they also want us to write very tight pre-nuptial agreements. Let's face it, our adult children have a lot to gain or lose from our choice of a late-in-life sweetheart. If you could marry someone who is healthy and wealthy, your children could logically imagine that your new spouse would be able to take care of both of you physically and financially. This could be a relief because it would take them off the hook of caring for you in your declining years. Choosing an ill or a poor mate would take your time and money away from them and your grandchildren.

Like it or not, our children are going to exercise their franchise and vote on any possible mate. My two daughters are not shy about speaking their minds after they have met someone I'm dating. Their questions always focus on my happiness. Do your adult children grade your date? You'll have to decide if they're looking out for your best interest or just their own. Those adult children who truly do care about your happiness will want to reserve judgment until they've at least had time to observe the enjoyment you get from the person you're dating.

When your grown children were just beginning to date, you probably had all sorts of advice to give them. Now they may have something to teach you. Some positive information can be gleaned from these volunteer coaches. I learned about on-line dating from my older daughter, and my younger daughter has made some very astute observations about my dates. I've decided to listen to them, thank them, and then decide for myself.

Dating Someone Who Is Already Taken

How could anyone do this with a clear conscience? It's easy. I met a man in a bar that always has a terrific band. The music was great, and I felt the urge to dance. I saw that most of the people there were younger, so I scanned the place to see if there were any older men available for dancing—and I found one. When the band played, "Give Me That Old Time Rock and Roll," I walked up to him and said, "I've been scanning the bar for someone my age, and this is such a great song. Would you like to dance?" We did, and the romance began. He was a great dancer, handsome, and very comfortable with himself and others. In short order, he got my name and number. The next day he called and asked me to meet him for dinner.

The dinner was filled with entertaining conversation. Topics included the story of his seventeen-year relationship that was never going to become a marriage or become a live-together situation. Upon hearing this, I was skeptical until he handed me the big flattery statement: "You're the only other woman I've asked out in seventeen years." Was he being honest? I figured he had told me about the seventeen-year relationship on our first date, so he must be an honest guy.

This became a crazy on again, off again love affair. I loved him, but he didn't love me or his long-term lady friend. It turned out that he loved himself first, his attraction to me second, and third, he wanted the ongoing stability that his seventeen-year relationship gave him.

I didn't consider myself a home wrecker, but now I began to understand how women who date married men must feel. They hope against all reason that the mutual attraction that exists between them will win out over the comfort of the tried-and-true. However, at our age, people usually choose comfort. Passion is lovely, but a social circle of long term couple friends is very comforting. As we get older, comfort sometimes trumps passion.

I have observed that many married couples stay together even though they despise one another. They don't want to split the assets, leave the house, or upset the adult children. Sometimes, one or both of them have lovers, but holidays and vacations find them enduring one another's company. Change is difficult—and risky.

Dating Someone Much Too Old for Me

If we LaterDaters™ begin a romance with someone more than ten years older than ourselves, the biggest problem that could result is that the relationship might work. We are living alone now and attempting to find someone to share our life. The average woman in this country lives six years longer than the average man. Do the math. If you are a sixty-year-old woman dating a seventy-year-old man and you decide to marry or live together, you are signing up for another sixteen years of being alone after he dies. These are just averages, and we know that life brings many surprises, but why risk it? Remember, my husband died at fifty-four, so I probably err on the side of caution here.

I was dating a Mr. Handsome/Intelligent/Charming/Enamored man. He was fourteen years older than me. I was impressed with him and our relationship began to get serious. It took me a few months to become realistic about this situation—he was just too old for me. I didn't want to become his nurse and being widowed in a few years didn't sound good either. If the tables were turned, would a sixty-one-year-old man date a seventy-five-year-old woman?

Unless you are looking for short-term companionship and maybe some additional financial security, I think people should date someone closer to their own age. Let's do the math on the relationship I got myself into. If we had married, I could plan on an average of twenty years of widowhood in my future. He was fourteen years older than I was and will probably live six years less than me. Does a sixty-one-year-old woman want to sign up for twenty more years of life alone? Think twice.

Why Do I Go Back to the Same Wrong Person Again, and Again, and…?

This problem is one that many men and women face—this person in your life who's always available but never wonderful. This person may be a past sweetheart who you would like to maintain as a friend, but this friend wants to return to sweetheart status. This friend can be relentless, and because you are lonely, you sometimes relent. Convenience is a hard habit to break, especially if you have control of the relationship. Yet remember, that you're not being fair to them, and you're misallocating dating time.

A sixty-five-year-old man loves me. This should be the beginning to a wonderful story, if only I loved him too. I think that he believes he can convince me that our life together would be great—if he just keeps trying. He finds excuses to call me, and when we do see one another, he seems fixated on our financial equality and how we could go to all the wonderful places in the world. He is financially well off, has a wide range of interests, is intellectually curious, and adventuresome.

What woman wouldn't want a man like this? What am I thinking? I am thinking about all the qualities he's missing: a quick sense of humor, social graces, and a knowledge of sensuality. So why do I continue to go back to him? I guess it's because I remember his good qualities and hold the unrealistic hope that this time he'll be funny and cuddly. Each time, I find that our relationship continues to be disappointing, and a breakup follows.

We are being manipulated by our hopes and dreams. He is hoping for a marriage with me who, in turn, is hoping he will become marriage material. Can I adjust my dreams to his reality? Can he adjust his reality to my dreams? I hope this see-saw romance can be balanced—or ended —and that we both live happily ever after.

Do Some Checking On the Person You Are Dating

There are many LaterDaters™ who do background checks on the people they are dating. They may use on-line services, information from friends, or even private detective services. Many of us have met people who misrepresented themselves in a variety of ways. If you have a feeling that the person you are dating is looking for something other than a great relationship, do some checking.

I was dating a handsome man who was retired and played lots of tennis. He had taken me out to eat four times. On the fourth date, he

CHAPTER ELEVEN 113

made it clear that it was time to move on to the next stage—intimacy. He had invested four dates worth of time and money, and I felt the pressure to go along with his suggestion. I avoided this mistake because I had done some checking.

It was easy to find out all about his fatal flaw because of his addiction to tennis. The Twin Cities of Minneapolis and St. Paul have about 3.5 million people, but it's a small town in many ways. I asked a few of my friends who were tennis players, and they filled me in on this man's negative qualities. The women I talked to even recommended other women to call for more information. All is fair in checking out dates—and certainly in checking out potential lovers!

CHAPTER TWELVE

♥

> I'm going to tell this creep exactly what I think of him.

> I'm going to tell this princess just where she can get off.

> In an argument, the best weapon is to hold your tongue.

Why and How to Say "Good-bye"

If It Isn't Working, Exit

If you have chosen to read this book, you probably had an occasion in your life when what initially seemed like a wonderful relationship took a turn for the worse. The purpose of this chapter is to look at the red flags that should have warned you there was trouble coming, then to instruct you how to get out fast and gracefully. Knowing these signs of incompatibility and knowing how to exit the relationship quickly will save you a lot of time—possibly years—that could have been used to find the great relationship you deserve. Time is precious—don't waste it on the wrong person.

Saying Good-bye after a Lengthy Relationship

In chapter six of this book, you were asked to check the qualities that you were looking for in a sweetheart. Are most of those qualities present in the person you are currently dating? Are some of them present in the person with whom you are currently having a long term, steady, and exclusive relationship? Are any of those qualities present? Are you currently using this person because you want some companionship or because the great sex makes up for a long list of missing qualities?

If any of these questions raise red flags in your mind, you may need to say good-bye to any person who lacks the characteristics you are looking for or has a different relationship goal from you. Have you been blindsided by your cave-person thinking? Is she beautiful; is he handsome, but lacking other good qualities? Is this person rich, but without any other good attributes?

Guys often end a heavy duty relationship by simply never calling that woman again. They avoid discussing the situation because they don't want to answer the "Why?" question. I think they believe they are really being kind with this silent treatment. A man may believe that the woman would be very hurt by his honesty, or he may just be a jerk. Remember that every town is a small town, and you don't want to be known as the town jerk! Women can be town jerks too. They accomplish this by not answering or returning phone calls. Breaking up a romance demands an actual conversation. We all deserve, at the least, an explanation. When you do that, begin by stating the good qualities of the person, then move on to your own goals.

If you decide to say good-bye to your steady, you need to plan ahead for a possible negative reaction from that person. The reaction you can expect will probably be directly proportional to how much the person cares for you. Both people hate that breakup moment. You have enjoyed one another and made plans for future times together. Your friends and relatives speak of you as a single unit—a couple. So this takes some courage. Choose a public place, a restaurant is best, where a tantrum would be unacceptable. Set it up so both of you have driven separately. Be kind to the point of telling small white lies. No one wants to hear brutal truth from someone with whom they shared a romance. Remember that news travels fast in every town, big or small, and if you are rude and crude in your breakup, the person you hurt could make your life miserable.

Once you are free from a mismatched relationship, you are free to start a more successful relationship. The rest of this chapter will address all the different ways single adults meet one another: friends/relatives, bars/coffee shops, activity clubs, singles dances, on-line, speed dating, dating services, personal ads, singles vacations, interest groups, or at your

CHAPTER TWELVE 117

place of work. How can you see the red flags at those initial meetings so that you will never have to do the potentially ugly breakup again?

The First Meeting

There are some things that just scream "No!" when we meet a new person. All of us have our own list of deal breakers. What human characteristics make future meetings a waste of your time and theirs? Slovenliness? Smoking? Self-centered chatter? If you are able to identify your deal breakers quickly, you will save yourself a lot of time and heartbreak by saying good-bye quickly.

I believe that we usually size one another up almost instantly and certainly in the first four minutes after meeting. This four-minute window of opportunity coincides with what business people report about how long it takes them to make a job interview decision. I have not included a lengthy list of deal breakers in this book because they'll be different for everyone. In that first four minutes I can easily determine if someone is well-groomed, well-dressed, well-spoken, well-mannered, and oh well, you get my four-minute picture. What are your deal breakers? How much time do you want to spend making small talk with someone who is never going to become a second date?

Being rude is not acceptable. Many men have told me that they peek through the coffee house window to see the lady they have been chatting with on-line before going in the building. If she doesn't measure up, they don't go in the door. Men are visual creatures by nature. They can't help themselves, and I don't fault them for this. Standing someone up, however, is rude. A twenty-minute cup of coffee is possible for everyone—you just need to know how to end it in that short amount of time. The trick is to start the conversation with an apology for the short amount of time you have for this meeting. Sounds like a job interview, doesn't it? You might need to pick up someone at the airport, or get to the bank before it closes, or get to the dealership for a car problem. Choose something that comes up unexpectedly, but needs your timely attention. If this reason employs a bit of fiction, then you have erred in pursuit of kindness.

The Set-up Failure—Say Good-bye

On those occasions when you are being set up for a date by friends or relatives, you will be able to find out lots of background information before you agree to the meeting. Remember that the other half of the set-up will have asked questions about you too. If your friends or relatives use descriptive words that indicate this prospective date is a charity case, you should be wary. What words? Devastated by the death or divorce of their spouse. Needs to get out more. You have the ability to cheer him or her up. Hasn't had a date in years. Is really trying to drink less. Listen for anything else that implies that they aren't a happy person, but could be needy. Do you want a romance or a project?

I am especially talking to you here if you are a woman. It is very difficult to change a person, no matter how caring and loving you may be. Trained therapists take years to make very small changes in their patients' outlook on life. You are looking for a sweetheart, not a patient. Having said that, I will add that we all have some baggage. If the person carrying that baggage is perfect for you in every way, you may be happy to help him or her carry it. What are those deal breakers for you: children at home, unemployment, cats, debt, or that very popular deal breaker—overweight or way underweight?

You will be able to find out all of these things before the fix-up. If you choose to be courteous to your friends and relatives, go ahead and meet this person. Be your usual charming self and watch for other red flags that would make a future date a waste of time for both of you. Ending a one-date fix-up is not difficult because no relationship has been established. As a man, you are not obligated to ask her out again. As a woman, you can politely make excuses for any future meetings.

The Bar or Coffeehouse Mishap—Say Good-bye

When you meet someone at a bar or a coffeehouse, beware of anyone who moves too quickly. Someone who seems pushy by standing or sitting too close, talking about personal topics too soon, or touching your hand, arm, waistline, or behind as if he or she is doing you a favor, is throwing up lots of red flags. Is it necessary to give someone a big squeezie hug to prove that you are warm-hearted, or would a handshake and a warm smile be friendly enough? Do not misinterpret this closeness as flattery. If the person wants to impress you, he or she will move slowly so that you are not offended. See the chapter on flirting to remind yourself that it, indeed, is a delicate dance and not a bulldozer event. People who talk about your, or their, financial situation may not only be rude, they may be calculating in every sense.

If this meeting has—in any way—become harassment, it is time to end the date. A public place such as a bar or coffeehouse may be a difficult venue to tell someone to take a flying leap, but it's better than a deserted country road. If the offending person isn't taking the hint by observing your appropriate behavior or by your requests for a change in their behavior, it is probably time to get out of there. The restroom excuse, with a quick detour to your car, should stop the harassment.

If you do meet someone at a bar or coffee shop who is the kind of quality person you are seeking, you may be tempted to hand out your name and phone number. It is safer to share your cell phone number or your email address. Your home phone number is a big clue to your address. If the person contacts you, your next date should be a meeting in a public place. Both of you should drive your own cars. If someone isn't happy with this cautious beginning to a relationship, you should consider that a red flag and say good-bye and good luck.

Saying Good-bye Involves the Entire Activity Club

Joining singles clubs that participate in specific activities, like skiing, tennis, golf, or dancing, etc. can be lots of fun and allow you to meet someone who shares at least one of your interests. My advice would be that you must truly enjoy this activity because the people in these clubs may have known each other for years. As a newcomer to the group, you should not expect to be greeted warmly. You are the competition for companionship. You will need to be the person who reaches out to the group. If you are not an extrovert by nature, this situation could be uncomfortable for you. If you do find a sweetheart in this group setting, my advice to you is to be very discreet. The rest of the group will notice any coupling that might occur, and you will be labeled as a couple long after the romance is over. This puts you at a distinct disadvantage for dating someone else in the club. Think of this as the smallest of small towns. Rumors fly, and breaking up had better be on the best of terms or you will be labeled as a _____ (fill in the blank) because you said good-bye to _____(fill in a name). Dating two people in the same singles group at the same time will always backfire. Don't do it.

Singles Dances Allow for Easy Good-byes

Singles dances present a perfect setting for meeting other single people who are looking for a chance to have some fun dancing and possibly even meeting that wonderful person they are seeking. A big red flag for both men and women is the person who wants to monopolize your dance card. Unless this person seems to be sent from heaven, it is wise to dance with as many people as possible—yes, the not-so-attractive ones too. You can always say, "Dancing with you has been so much fun, would you please save me a dance later in the evening?"

Another red flag for women is the groper. This guy thinks that your consent to dance with him gives him some temporary property rights. He puts his hands on your behind, or my most disgusting form of flattery, he makes it physically evident to you that he is attracted to you by pressing his erect member against you. Eek! What to do about that sort of inappropriate behavior? Place some distance between the two of you and remind him that dancing should not be so hard.

While you are having fun at a singles dance, remember not to turn into a red flag yourself. Don't drink alcoholic beverages because you are driving, and you want to keep your wits about you. No one is attracted to someone who has overindulged in alcohol. Don't sit with a group of other women or men far away from the action or you will be out of the playing field. Drive by yourself so that you are not controlled by a friend's schedule. If you are a woman who is at ease with asking a man to dance, go ahead and ask, but remember that men usually want to do the asking. Don't ask the same man a second time. Let him do the asking—or not.

On-line Meetings May Deserve a Good-bye

Using on-line dating sites is very efficient and a growing social phenomenon. Match.com started in 1995 and has a huge database. The over fifty group is the fastest growing segment on that site (Juarez 2006). Some of the people who use on-line services lie about themselves. These lies usually include a younger age, more height for men, less weight for women, and photos that are years old or retouched. To protect yourself from more serious misrepresentations, be sure to design an on-line name that doesn't hint of your real name. Your profile should not use words like sensual, lover, desires physical intimacy. A person reading these words in your profile will probably interpret them as a sexual invitation. Do you want to be held to that invitation after having shared a single cup of coffee?

So, there you are in that neutral meeting place that has taken four emails to determine, and you are asking yourself, "Why me and why him or her?" At first sight you knew this person was misrepresented in the profile you read. You could barely recognize him or her as the same person whose photo you saw on-line. If the photo was not on-line, that was already a red flag. You should have requested a photo before agreeing to meet. The person's stated weight and height might have been in some other unit of measure. How much time do you want to spend with a person who has obviously misrepresented themself?

Speed Dating Requires a Quick Good-bye—or a Big Hello

Speed dating events are great. You don't have to make up a reason to say good-bye because a little bell is going to ring every seven minutes and both of you are required to say good-bye so that each of you can meet the next person in circulation. Wonderful! Each couple makes small talk for seven minutes and sizes each other up. That's plenty of time to decide if you would like to spend more time with someone in the future. At the end of the evening. everyone turns in the names of those people they found interesting. All the lists are compared, and you receive an email the next day telling you about your mutual matches. Speed dating events for people over fifty are hard to find, but you can search on-line for your vicinity. It will be worth your time. You will meet up to twenty possible dates in the space of two hours.

Dating Services Provide Good-bye Screening

Dating services, whether It's Just Lunch or Together, or any of the others that are listed in your yellow pages, give you an opportunity to check out the person before you meet them. These dating services can be pricey, so be sure you know what you are buying before you sign on the line. These services have professional matchmakers who choose people they think will be perfect for you. Both of you have a chance to reject one another before you even meet for the first time. You will meet in a public place and, hopefully, you will have an enjoyable first date. If you see behaviors that are on your personal red flag list, you can avoid future dates easily enough. Men don't call and women can be busy with other events.

Personal Ads Seek Hello, but May Deserve a Good-bye

Personal ads in various types of publications are used by singles of all ages to meet one another. Red flags are built into the words that people choose to describe themselves and the relationship they are seeking. If a personal ad sounds creepy, you can assume the author is creepy. A well-written ad may deserve your response and possibly, a meeting. Remember the rules: meet in a public place and only share your cell number or your email address, not your home phone number or address. If your personal list of red flags starts waving, don't ignore it. People are usually showing their best behavior on a first date. If that's the best they can do, what would the worst look like? Surprise. He or she seems terrific. I think the second date should also be a meeting at a public place, with both of you driving separately.

CHAPTER THIRTEEN

Better Living Through Chemistry

"Sex truly is wasted on the young. They may have the equipment and the energy, but they don't have the experience," says sex therapist Lonnie Barback.

Recreational Drugs

Many of us LaterDaters™ lived through the first sexual revolution with the help of chemicals. I'm not referring to the illegal ones; I'm talking about that little pill that helped us control when and if we had children—that wonder of the 1960s, the birth control pill. That little pill allowed us to enjoy sex free from the fear of an unwanted pregnancy. And now chemistry has come to help our sex lives once again. The 1990s and Bob Dole brought improved solutions to erectile dysfunction problems. The 1990s also saw a wide variety of solutions to menopausal symptoms, including lack of sexual desire. The drug companies became very creative when they saw the huge market created when the first Baby Boomers turned fifty in the mid-1990s.

Ladies First: Sex, Drugs, and Hot Flashes (the Good Kind)

The average age for a woman to experience menopause is fifty-one. At that time they experience a dramatic change in many hormones in their bodies. Some women—20 to 30 percent—don't experience unpleasant side effects from these changes, but for the majority of us, all hell breaks loose. Our complaints start with the inconvenience of irregular periods and builds to daytime hot flashes then night sweats that keep us awake and cranky because we are exhausted from lack of sleep. Women may experience vaginal and urinary problems during this time of their lives. To make us feel even less attractive, we usually gain some weight and some wrinkles while losing some hair.

When women begin to experience menopause, their conversations sound something like this: " I can't stand to be dripping wet anymore; I'm taking hormones," or "I've got a history of breast cancer in my family, and I'm not going to take the risk," or "It's supposed to be good for your heart; I'm going to use hormones," or "I'm in such a bad mood all the time, bring on the drugs!"

The very personal choice of whether or not to treat your menopausal symptoms is complicated by the endless variety of choices: Premarin, Prempro, bioidenticals derived from plants, herbal remedies, and even custom compounds that are not FDA approved. Women agonize over the choices and should talk about these choices with a trusted personal physician. Besides talking to your doctor, I believe you should do some research on your own. I started reading about menopause eight years before I experienced it because I was really looking forward to not having my period. After all my research, I ended up making my decision by asking my gynecologist what his wife took for menopausal symptoms. Be sure to do your own research: talk to your friends about their experiences, do some library research about the issues, and check out web sites. You need to know your options so you can have an informed discussion with your care provider about how you want to treat your menopausal symptoms.

In 2002, the FDA added warning labels to hormone replacement therapy (HRT) products warning women to take the lowest dose for the shortest time possible. Dr. Isadore Rosenfeld reported in the October

9, 2005, *Duluth News Tribune* that "Postmenopausal women who have been taking HRT for two years or more are at slightly increased risk of stroke—as well as for breast cancer and heart attacks." When I read this sentence, I focus on the "slightly increased risk," but you may find this statement alarming. You may want to seek more information to compare the potential value against the potential risks. If you are currently using menopausal medications, you would be wise to again reassess whatever you are using every year when you go to see your gynecologist for your Pap smear.

If you are dating with the goal of developing an intimate relationship, you may be experiencing a decreased libido because of your decreased hormone levels. If you are in a loving relationship and having frequent and good sex with your partner, your desire can be maintained into and through menopause. For those of us over fifty and dating, our decreasing hormone levels are probably teaming up with decreasing sexual activity. The result is a decline in vaginal health. The walls of the vagina and labia become thinner, less elastic, and more prone to infection. Lubrication during intercourse takes longer than it did before menopause. HRT to the rescue. There are some side effects of HRT that we need to discuss—the sexual advantages.

Estrogen can help maintain vaginal health, and progesterone seems to calm the women who are worried about breast cancer, but there is one hormone out there that can be a big boost to your libido. Testosterone: it's not just for men anymore. Healthy pre-menopausal women have testosterone in their bodies, albeit about one-tenth the level of men. Replacing estrogen has very little effect on women's sexual interest, but combine it with testosterone, and women have an increase in desire and arousal. By the time women have reached fifty, sixty, or seventy, we've got lots of good things going for us. We know what we want sexually, we finally know how to ask for it, and with estrogen and progesterone we have healthy sexual organs. If we take testosterone, we gain desire, and we are easily aroused. Combine all these qualities and you should be able to have hot flashes all right—the kind we all enjoy and never complain about (Hales 1999).

Ask your doctor about all the kinds of treatment available for menopausal symptoms. Then get a second and third opinion. My decision was based on my research, and it may not be right for you. I take estrogen, progesterone, and testosterone. This regimen may not be your decision. I chose it with my doctor's advice. I also used the information I found in a book titled *Just Like A Woman*, by Dianne Hales. It stated, "Epidemiological studies have shown it [estrogen] to be so beneficial to women's other systems that, in statistical analyses, it extends life span by an estimated 20 to 37 percent. Estrogen seems to boost spirit by stimulating the production of receptors that respond to serotonin a key regulator of mood. In women, low levels of estrogen and serotonin may be linked to depression and other mental disorders. Lower testosterone in women causes a loss of libido, as well as a decline in sexual fantasies and intercourse" (Hales 1999). HRT works very well for me, and I consider it part of a healthy lifestyle choice, along with exercise, a daily vitamin pill, and a healthy diet. But, I'm not a medical doctor. I'm only a researcher.

Gentlemen Second: Sex, Drugs, and Getting It Up

As a male over the age of fifty reading this book, you are experiencing a very slow decline in testosterone levels in your body. Testosterone is the libido hormone and stimulates sexual desire. You will never again have to stand up in front of the class to give a book report holding a notebook over your erect member. You probably don't even carry a notebook on movie or dinner dates—but if you're one of the lucky ones, you know that popcorn boxes and restaurants with tablecloths can come in very handy.

What I hear from gentlemen over fifty is: "I never put myself in an intimate situation if there's any doubt in my mind that I will be able to get an erection." The fear of an unwanted erection has turned into the fear of not being able to achieve an erection. The same event that embarrassed you in junior high school can become your most desired experience when you are over fifty, single, and looking for an intimate relationship.

Let's start at the beginning: What causes an erection? Natural erections are complex events that require the central nervous system and the relaxation of the trabecular and arterial smooth muscle cells of the penis. Erections start in your brain for lots of different reasons—for example, a visual stimulus or an erotic memory. The resulting chemicals that are sent to the penis result in more blood flowing into your penis and less flowing out. In your glory days, all that was required to achieve and maintain an erection was a willing partner who seemed attractive at the moment. But, as my mother always told me, "Getting old is the shits." You may be finding that your partner has to be attractive in very specific ways, and you may even require a partner who uses correct grammar before you start working your way to the bedroom. And I do mean working! Such as," How many dinners, flowers, and drinks is this going to take before I can get her to the bedroom?"

As the years go by, you can only expect your testosterone levels to slowly get lower and lower (sorry about that second use of the word lower). Remember, as your testosterone level is lowering, your desire to have sex is also lowering. In the U.S., 10 percent of males at the age of fifty are impotent. By the age of sixty, that number has increased to 20 percent. When men reach the age of seventy, 30 percent are experiencing erectile dysfunction. Men over the age of eighty have a 75 percent rate of ED (Walker 1994). These numbers result in an estimated fifteen to thirty million American men with erectile problems. Many of these men are too embarrassed to tell their doctors about it and, unfortunately, many doctors do not ask about the problem. If you're over fifty, experiencing ED and you want to be in an intimate relationship, you need to solve this problem. Go to see your urologist and be frank about your situation.

Lowered testosterone levels are only one of the possible causes of erectile dysfuntion. There are psychological causes such as anxiety and stress. Physical causes, however, are believed to be responsible for 90 percent of all impotence problems. Those physical problems include stroke, prostate surgery, or spinal cord injury. The majority of the physical reasons for erectile dysfunction fall under the category of physical diseases that cause vascular malfunction. These diseases include arteriosclerosis, high cholesterol, hardening of the arteries, diabetes, and multiple sclerosis (LaHaye 2000).

Do not despair. Modern medical science and Bob Dole have made it possible for you to need that notebook again. Since losing the presidential election in 1996, Bob Dole, the former U.S. senator from Kansas, has become the first spokesperson for erectile dysfunction, formerly referred to as impotence and now termed ED. Most of us hadn't heard the term erectile dysfunction at that time. Apparently, many men had experienced it, but few of them knew about a medication that could reverse the problem.

There are currently three popular erectile disfunction drugs on the market: Viagra is effective for about four hours, but most effective after one hour. Cialis can be effective within forty-five minutes and may work for up to thirty-six hours. Levitra can work within twenty minutes and is said to be effective for four hours. None of these drugs cause an erection by themselves; they all require sexual stimulation to be effective. There has been a reported 65–72 percent "very happy" analysis of these drugs (LaHaye 2000). All of these drugs need a doctor's prescription and come with a long list of "do not use if" certain medical conditions are present or certain reactions happen. These are serious drugs, and hopefully, they will get you in to see a doctor for a complete physical. An Australian survey of one thousand men and women between sixty-five and ninety-three indicated that two-thirds believed sexual relations are an important part of intimacy in later life but 62 percent were unaware of the adverse effects that prescription medication or depression can have on the human sex drive (Gross, Zenith, Harken 2000).

Your doctor may advise against using ED drugs if you have certain medical conditions. ED drugs may cause you to experience some of the following side effects: headache, heartburn, upset stomach, runny nose, diarrhea, urinary tract infections, or blurred vision. The greatest danger is using ED drugs with other drugs—specifically, prescription drugs that lower blood pressure. Mixing erectile dysfuntion drugs with drugs that lower your blood pressure can be lethal.

There are older methods that you could try. These methods do not receive the advertising attention of Viagra, Cialis, and Levitra, but for those men who have medical conditions that do not tolerate the ED pills, these older alternatives may work for you. These alternatives include a penile prosthesis, the vacuum pump, and injection therapy.

In the late 1970s and early 1980s, the only dependable treatment for impotent men was the implantation of a penile prosthesis. There are basically two types of implants: the insertion of a bendable rod into the penis, or the much more complicated and costly insertion of a cylinder into the penis that is pumped up with fluid from a reservoir that is placed under the abdominal muscle.

In the 1970s, the vacuum erection device was introduced. These should be obtained from your doctor, not from a sex toy catalogue. This is often the first treatment tried, and it works for two-thirds of those suffering from ED (LaHaye 2000). It works by removing air from a cylinder around the penis, thereby increasing blood flow. The blood is then kept in the penis with a constriction ring It has a thirty-minute maximum use. However, some men have found this method to be disappointing or cumbersome.

In the 1980s, an injection therapy was introduced. The product and instructions should be available from your urologist. The intracavernous-injection therapy with alprostadil (a synthetic prostaglandin E 1 low) is injected into the loose skin of the scrotal sac at the base of the penis to produce an erection. It almost guarantees at least a thirty-minute erection.

Today, men have many choices to overcome erectile dysfunction. If you are experiencing this problem, it is very important that you see your doctor for a complete physical and, for heaven's sake, speak frankly about ED. It is not an issue that should remain under the covers any longer. Be a real man and be pro-active about this medical condition.

We Need a Joke Here!

There is more money being spent on breast implants and ED medication today than on Alzheimer's research. This means that by 2040, there should be a large elderly population with perky boobs and big erections and absolutely no recollection of what to do with them.

Good Sex Requires Good Communication and the Other Kind of Chemistry

Many men and women over the age of fifty can overcome sexual dysfunction without drugs of any kind. The old fashioned ways to achieve arousal still work: communication and masturbation. Drugs are a wonderful assistance to those of us who are over fifty, but they don't necessarily result in a satisfying sexual relationship. Women can remain interested in being sexually active with hormone replacement or with the luxury of a trusting long term monogamous relationship.

Our discussions should include the M word. Don't underestimate the pleasure of masturbation. Most of us learned about our sexual selves by masturbating. We all still have the right to use masturbation either alone or with our sweetie. However, neither hormones, masturbation, or ED drugs can guarantee a satisfying sex life. We need to be attracted to our partners (that other kind of chemistry), and then we need to be able to communicate our sexual needs. If we are comfortable enough to be naked and sexually active with a person, then why is it that we are still unable to talk about sex with that person?

It's those pious Puritans (our own colonial taliban) who make this sex talk difficult. Get over it. Ask your partner what sexual activities are most effective for them to achieve orgasm. We can't read each other's minds. If this is all too blunt for you, think of it as ordering from a menu at a restaurant. Would you ever be able to instinctively know what your sweetheart is going to order for dinner? Would they be able to predict what kind of food you are craving that evening? Don't we all want to be good lovers? We need to stop and ask for directions.

Talking about sex isn't easy, but it really delivers better sex. If you are interested enough in this person to share your body with them, my guess would be that you want this sexual experience to be good for both of you. For those of you who want to know how to sexually satisfy your partner, there are many books to read at the library or the bookstore. I would recommend that women read *Sex Tips for Straight Women from a Gay Man* by Dan Anderson and Maggie Berman. Men should read the last three chapters of *What Women Want Men to Know* by Barbara DeAngelis, Ph.D.

CHAPTER FOURTEEN

♥

STDs, Yes, This Means You

Looking for love in too many faces can lead to sexually transmitted diseases. Most adults over fifty still enjoy sex and want to be involved in a relationship that is sexually satisfying. This can usually be done safely in a marriage or monogamous relationship, but the millions of us who are dating need to be very alert to the alarming facts about STDs in the over fifty population. Women over the age of fifty are especially at risk because their vaginal walls are thinning and more easily infected. I'm sure none of us want a sexually transmitted disease, but our behavior needs to prove it. Two adults usually date one another because they are attracted to one another, and that attraction often times leads to sexual activity. An older sexual partner has had more time to experience more sexual partners and, therefore, more opportunity to contract a STD.

According to the July/August 2005 issue of *AARP: The Magazine*, the following numbers prove that people over fifty are very misinformed about HIV/AIDS. A study of 514 women over the age of fifty was conducted at Emory University in Atlanta. It reported the following: only 13 percent believed that condoms were effective in preventing HIV/AIDS, 63 percent said it could be transmitted by kissing, 50 percent thought vasectomies provided protection, and 44 percent believed abstinence was not at all or only somewhat effective in preventing HIV.

Is it any wonder that HIV/AIDS is a growing problem in people over the age of fifty? During the years 2000 through 2003, thirty thousand people over the age of forty-five were diagnosed with HIV. This thirty thousand represents 23 percent of the total cases diagnosed during those three years. These cases were not all the result of male-to-male contact or injection drug use. Heterosexual sex led to 30 percent of the total cases.

If you're not willing to die for love, you will need to use condoms. This means you, this means me, and this means all of us. Condoms are a necessity!

PART FOUR

Your LaterDating™ Plan

"Even if you're on the right track, you'll get run over if you just sit there." Will Rogers

CHAPTER FIFTEEN

Your Dating Plan

There is never a shortage of people who want to advise others about how to succeed in life and love. All of us have made mistakes in our lives, so we are usually willing to listen to anyone who seems to have the right stuff. You may have changed to a better financial planner, a church that was a better fit, read books about how a strong vision of your goal will make it happen, or even used astrologers and mystics to help you find the answers. Good news, you don't have to take dating advice from mystics or your peers who haven't been single since they were nineteen.

This book has attempted to provide honest answers to common LaterDater™ questions. My hope is that the information and stories in this book gave you a clearer picture of the LaterDating™ world. In chapter six, you learned about the qualities other people in your gender and age group are seeking in a dating partner, and you were asked to clarify the qualities you would like to have in someone you date. Chapter seven elaborated on the most effective ways other LaterDaters™ found someone to date. Chapter eight examined the relationship goals of two hundred LaterDaters™ based on gender, age, and times married. You were then asked to determine your own goals. Chapter nine asked the hard question about your own qualifications Would others want to date you? You now have what it takes to make a successful dating plan. Use the power!

Your Personal Plan for Dating Success

Identifying Your Relationship Goals

1. What kind of relationships are you seeking? See the list on page 74.
   _____
   _____

2. Looking at table 8.1 on page 76, write down the percent of opposite sex people who want the same type of relationships that you chose.
   _____

3. Check out table 8.2 on page 77, write down the percent of people in your acceptable age categories who share your relationship goals.___
   _____

4. Are your relationship choices popular with others?_____

5. Are you willing to change your relationship goals?_____

Finding a Date

6. What have you tried in the last year in an attempt to find someone to date? See page 60. _____
   _____

7. What attempts proved successful? _____
   _____

8. By looking at the three tables in chapter seven on pages 60, 63, and 64, decide what you're going to try next to find someone that you want to date. Did you summarize those on page 71? Where and how will you find dating success? Write your answers here._____
   _____
   _____

9. Do you have the time, energy, and resources to date a lot of people until you find the perfect person?_____

10. Would you be willing to pay a dating service to help you find people to date, knowing there are no guarantees?_____
_____

11. What is limiting your dating success? Refer to chapter nine, "Would You Date You?" Remember that similar interests is the quality everyone seems to be seeking. After that, men look for physically attractive and women chose a close combination of intelligent/kind/financially stable._____
_____
_____

12. Knowing that it is difficult to radically change your appearance, your I.Q., or your financial situation, what could you reasonably do to make yourself more date-able? _____
_____

13. On pages 91 and 92, you rated your dating self. Jot down a few words to remind yourself how you are going to behave on your next date._____
_____

14. Flirting can be initiated by either men or women. Describe how you could flirt with someone without offending them or embarrassing yourself. See chapter ten starting on page 97. _____
_____
_____

Have Fun Dating

15. Remember someone doesn't have to be perfect to be a fun date. Are you willing to shorten your list of qualities you're seeking and also your list of deal-breakers? List them here._____
_____
_____

16. How will you keep a positive outlook during the ups and downs of the dating process? Make up a slogan to keep a positive dating attitude and write it here. _____
_____

If you need some slogan help, start with these phrases.

Lots of LaterDaters™ chose the word fun because_____
I can make any date fun because _____
Dates grow on trees because_____
Forty million potential LaterDaters™ are_____

I Have Saved the Best Story for Last

While I was handing out my survey at a Matched Singles Tennis Club, I met a woman, Chris, who wanted to share her ninety-eight-year-old father's story.

Chris' story: "He just moved into assisted living. Though he's not dating per se, that desire for love and companionship is the same and just as strong. I'm sending a photo so you can see the energy between the two. Hope this will be of interest to you."

His story: "After moving into assisted living and being here about two weeks I joined the birthday celebration of a woman who was turning 102! We immediately took a strong liking to each other. She is so alert, has a good memory, likes to laugh and snuggle close. She is somewhat hard of hearing so I have plenty of opportunity to lean real close. She even has her own teeth. The more I learn about her, the more I feel she's a wonder. A lot of people half her age are not that alert. She is truly amazing."

**Remember,
we are all amazing in some way,
and we all deserve love and companionship.**

APPENDIX

TABLE 7.2B DATING METHODS <u>TRIED</u> BY AGE GROUPS

Age Groups ▶ Methods ▼	50-55 N=45	56-60 N=57	65-65 N=47	66-70 N=30	71-75 N=13	75+ N=8
Friends & Relatives	64%	63%	64%	57%	46%	50%
Bars & Coffee	47%	35%	35%	20%	15%	0%
Joining Activities	73%	60%	54%	47%	62%	63%
Singles Dances	69%	60%	53%	37%	62%	25%
On-line Services	56%	39%	53%	27%	8%	0%
Speed Dating	22%	25%	30%	3%	8%	0%
Dating Services	22%	18%	21%	7%	8%	0%
Personal Ads	31%	21%	32%	17%	38%	0%
Singles Vacations	9%	11%	11%	0%	8%	0%
Interest Groups	51%	44%	17%	30%	46%	50%
Other Methods	13%	12%	6%	13%	15%	13%

N = number of respondents in an age category.
Some respondents chose more than one category.

TABLE 7.3B DATING METHODS <u>TRIED</u> BY TIMES MARRIED

Times Married ▶ Methods ▼	Married 0 times N=30	Married 1 time N=123	Married 2 times N=43	Married 3 times N=4
Friends & Relatives	70%	54%	70%	100%
Bars & Coffee	53%	28%	35%	10%
Joining Activities	53%	65%	49%	50%
Singles Dances	65%	52%	60%	50%
On-line Services	23%	42%	42%	100%
Speed Dating	23%	19%	21%	25%
Dating Services	13%	15%	23%	0%
Personal Ads	23%	24%	30%	25%
Singles Vacations	13%	7%	9%	0%
Interest Groups	30%	40%	35%	50%
Other Methods	10%	12%	12%	0%

N = number of respondents.
Some respondents chose many methods.

BIBLIOGRAPHY

Anderson, Dan, and Berman, Maggie. *Sex Tips for Straight Women from a Gay Man.* New York: HarperCollins, 1997.

Bair, Deirde. *Calling It Quits; Late-Life Divorce And Starting Over,* New York: Random House, 2007.

DeAngelis, Barbara Ph.D. *What Women Want Men to Know,* New York: Hyperion, 2002.

Fisher, Helen E. *Anatomy of Love.* New York: Norton & Company, 1992: 20–21 and 31–32.

Foley, Sallie. *AARP: The Magazine,* Nov/Dec 2005.

Frances, Peter. "Well Enough Alone." *American Demographics,* Nov 1, 2003.

Gottesman, Nancy. "HIV Over 50," *AARP: The Magazine,* Washington D.C.: July/August 2005: 58.

Gross, Zenith, Henkin. *Seasons of the Heart: Men and Women Talk about Love, Sex, and Romance after 60.* Novato California: New World Library, 2000.

Hales, Dianne. *Just Like A Woman.* Charlotte North Carolina: Bantam, 1999: 76–80.

Juarez, Vanessa. **www.findlovehere.com**, *Newsweek,* February 2006: 60.

Kaiser, Donald H., and Kausler, Barry C. *Encyclopedia of Aging, Health, Mind, and Behavior.* Illinois: University of Illinois Press, 1996.

LaHaye, Tim F. and Beverly. *The Act of Marriage.* Grand Rapids, MI: Zondervan Publishing House, 2000: 109–110, 113–114.

Lynch, James J. Ph.D. *A Cry Unheard: New Insights into the Medical Consequences of Loneliness.* Baltimore Maryland: Bancroft Press, 2000.

Mahoney, Sarah. "Seeking Love". *AARP: The Magazine,* July/August 2005.

Mead, Margaret. *Male and Female.* Charlotte, NC: Dell Publishing Co., 1949: 247–248.

Roden, Margaret. *Love and Romance over the Life Cycle.* American Sociological Association, 1985.

Walker, Morton. *Sexual Nutrition.* New York: Instant Improvement, 1994: 12.

Warren, Neil Clark, Ph.D. *Date…or Soul Mate?* Nashville, Tennessee: Thomas Nelson, Inc., 2002: 173.

U.S. Census of 2005, Table 55. Marital Status of the Population by Sex and Age.

ABOUT THE AUTHOR

Linda Fraser, M.A., is a professional educator and presenter currently living in Minneapolis, Minnesota. She has written curriculum for and worked with both high school and adult learners. She currently consults for Minneapolis Public Schools. She is also a member of the Loft Literary Center in Minneapolis.

Unexpectedly widowed, Linda entered the world of LaterDating™. She quickly learned that the dating world for people over fifty, like herself, was drastically different from what she remembered or anticipated. The advice of her two single daughters was often not all that applicable. Her numerous coupled friends were unable to relate. Conversations with other single people over fifty included many more questions than answers. These questions, the stories shared by her peers, and her own experiences over seven years of LaterDating™ inspired this book.

Fraser understood that writing a valid survey and correctly analyzing the results would require more expertise than she possessed, so she got help. Her older daughter, Molly Coyne, earned a Ph.D. in Evaluation, and Molly made sure Linda's survey work was accurate and the statistics were correct.

The author welcomes your comments or questions. Email her at **Linda@FindingYourSweetieAfter50.com.**